From Information to Decision Making:

New Challenges for Effective Citizenship

Margaret A. Laughlin
H. Michael Hartoonian
Norris M. Sanders
Editors

National Council for the Social Studies

President
Donald O. Schneider
University of Georgia
Athens, Georgia

President - Elect
Mary McFarland
Parkway School District
Chesterfield, Missouri

Vice President
Fred Risinger
Social Studies Development
 Center and ERIC/ChESS
Indiana University
Bloomington, Indiana

Executive Director
Frances Haley
Washington, D.C.

Associate Executive Director
Sara Wallace
Washington, D.C.

Board of Directors
Linda Biemer
Andrea M. Coulter
Judith M. Finkelstein
Jesus Garcia
H. Michael Hartoonian
Rachel Hicks
Richard Kraft
Tedd Levy
William Marks
Margit McGuire
Paul H. Pangrace
Denny Schillings
Paul R. Shires
Karen Todorov
Jan L. Tucker
Vickie Weiss

Ex Officio
Richard Theisen

Director of Publications
Salvatore J. Natoli
Washington, D.C.

Publications Committee
William W. Wilen, Chair
Virginia A. Atwood
Margaret A. Carter
Wentworth Clarke
Denny Schillings
Mary Jane Turner
David A. Welton

Ex Officio
Frances Haley
Salvatore J. Natoli
Fred Risinger, Vice President
James E. Davis, Chair, *Social Education* Editorial Committee

Library of Congress Catalog Card Number 89–61568
ISBN 0–87986–058–0
Copyright © 1989 by
NATIONAL COUNCIL FOR THE SOCIAL STUDIES
3501 Newark Street N.W., Washington, D.C. 20016

Table of Contents

About the Authors — v

Preface — vii

Chapter 1. Educating Students for an Information Age — 1
Margaret A. Laughlin
Introduction; Critics of Information Technology; Social Studies in an Information Age; An Overview

Chapter 2. Using Data in Elementary Social Studies Programs — 11
Rosemary G. Messick and June R. Chapin
Fitting the Task to the Child; Topics for Study; Data-Generating Strategies; Summary

Chapter 3. Strategic Thinking in the Social Studies — 19
Kathryn A. Koch
Topic and Question Selection; Gathering Data; Recording Data; Understanding Data; Reporting and Using Information; Data Strategies; Conclusion

Chapter 4. Civic Decision Making in an Information Age — 31
Richard C. Remy
Public Policy Decisions in the Modern Age; A Decision-making Model for the Information Age; Practical Classroom Applications

Chapter 5. Using Census Data in Elementary and Secondary Social Studies Programs: A Timely Example — 39
George Dailey and Leah Engelhardt
Fact Finder for the Nation; Real-World Information; Census Data, Census Concepts, and Classroom Objectives; The Decennial Census as a Classroom Focus; 1990 Census Education Project

Chapter 6. Social Mathematics — 51
H. Michael Hartoonian
Introduction; Quantitative Concepts; Social Mathematics and Social Studies Curriculum; Social Mathematics and Social Studies Instruction; Conclusion

Chapter 7. Tools for Social Mathematics — 65
James G. Lengel
In the Early Grades; In the Later Grades; The Role of the Computer; More Lesson Ideas

Chapter 8. **Social Problem Solving Using Data Bases** — **71**
Norris M. Sanders
Common Features of Data Base Programs; Classroom Equipment for Serious Data Processing; Social Data Processing in the Curriculum; Teacher Preparation

Chapter 9. **School Media Programs in the Information Age** — **81**
Daniel Callison
National Guidelines; Teaching Methods for the Information Age; The New Information Technologies; Research on Secondary School Student On-line Information Use

Chapter 10. **Locating and Using ERIC and Other Data-Collection Sources** — **93**
C. Frederick Risinger
Computers, Data Bases, and the Social Studies; ERIC—The Data Base for Educators; How Social Studies Teachers Can Use the ERIC Data Base

Chapter 11. **How School Textbook Publishers View the Information Age** — **101**
Cameron S. Moseley
(A fictitious interview of a publisher who presents views held by many leaders in the textbook industry.)

Chapter 12. **Human Dimensions of the Information Age** — **111**
Margaret A. Laughlin, H. Michael Hartoonian, and Norris M. Sanders
The Curriculum; Instructional Materials and Equipment; The Teacher

About the Authors

June R. Chapin Dr. Chapin is Professor of Education at the College of Notre Dame in Belmont, California. Over the years, she has written several textbooks for students and has published widely in professional social studies journals. She has been active in the California Council for the Social Studies and the National Council for the Social Studies, as well as in the College and University Faculty Association of NCSS. She makes frequent presentations at various social studies programs.

Daniel Callison Daniel Callison is Assistant Professor and Associate Dean of the School of Library and Information Science at Indiana University, Bloomington. He has written extensively about changes in school and library programs in an Information Age and is an active member of the American Library Association.

George Dailey George Dailey is Coordinator of the 1990 Census Education Project, sponsored by the United States Bureau of the Census. Dailey is a coeditor of a special section of a forthcoming issue of *Social Education* related to teaching about the 1990 Census. The United States Census Bureau has recently published *Census Education Project 1990* for use by social studies teachers.

Leah Engelhardt Dr. Engelhardt was recently appointed Department Chair of Teacher Education at Purdue University–Calumet in Hammond, Indiana. Prior to going to Indiana, Dr. Engelhardt was Professor of Education at Mississippi State University. She has served as a consultant to the Bicentennial Project of the United States Constitution in Oklahoma and is a consultant to the 1990 Census Bureau Education Project.

H. Michael Hartoonian Michael Hartoonian is Social Studies Supervisor for the Wisconsin Department of Public Instruction and is Adjunct Professor at the University of Wisconsin–Madison. Dr. Hartoonian has worked with social studies leaders in numerous states and districts across the United States. He is a frequent speaker and author of numerous articles. At present, he is serving on the Board of Directors of the National Council for the Social Studies. He is coauthoring a secondary social studies textbook with Margaret Laughlin, *Challenges in Teaching Secondary Social Studies*.

Kathryn A. Koch Dr. Koch is Assistant Professor of Education at the University of Wisconsin–Green Bay, where she specializes in teaching reading methods to elementary and secondary teacher-preparation students and offers a variety of graduate classes for experienced teachers. In addition to an active writing schedule, Dr. Koch devotes much of her time to speaking at professional conferences and conducting seminars for teachers and parents. She is on the National Board of Advisers for the Christian Educators Association and a member of several professional reading associations.

Margaret A. Laughlin Margaret Laughlin is Associate Professor of Education at the University of Wisconsin–Green Bay where she teaches both elementary and secondary social studies methods classes for students preparing to be teachers. In addition, she teaches graduate courses in curriculum and foundations. At UWGB, she is also the Director for the Center for Economic Education. She is currently working on a social studies textbook *Challenges in Teaching Secondary Social Studies* (to be published by Harcourt Brace Jovanovich), which she is coauthoring with Michael Hartoonian. She has recently been asked to serve as chair for the Committee to Revise the NCSS Curriculum Guidelines.

James Lengel James Lengel is Education Technology Consultant for Apple Computer. His social studies career began in the elementary and secondary classroom and included 13 years at the Vermont Education Department as Social Studies Consultant and as the state's Deputy Commissioner of Education. He recently coauthored *Using Computers in the Social Studies* with Diane Kendall and Howard Budin, published by Teachers College Press. Lengel can be reached through Apple Computer, 171 Locke Drive, Marlborough, Massachusetts 01752.

Rosemary G. Messick Rosemary Messick is Professor of Education at San Jose State University in California where her interests are in elementary and early childhood education and the use of computers. She has traveled widely and has taught and conducted research in Brazil. Dr. Messick is active in the California Council for the Social Studies and the National Council for the Social Studies where she has presented a variety of programs of interest to social studies teachers.

Cameron S. Moseley Cameron Moseley entered publishing in 1941 as an elementary and high school textbook salesperson for Roe, Peterson. After serving in the armed services, he joined Harcourt Brace & Company (now Harcourt Brace Jovanovich) as a high school and college salesperson and promotion writer. During his 24 years with HBJ, he held a wide variety of marketing, administrative, and editorial positions and was also active in industry-association affairs. The "universal ownership label" that appears in all textbooks was his conception. From 1967 to 1970, he was senior vice president and director of the school department, and a director of HBJ. Since 1971, Moseley has been head of Moseley Associates, Inc., management consultants to the publishing industry.

Richard C. Remy Richard Remy is Director of the Mershon Center at Ohio State University. The center has produced a variety of curriculum materials related to citizenship education and, most recently, materials for teaching about security in a nuclear age. Dr. Remy has made numerous presentations at conferences and workshops across the country and has published widely on topics related to social studies and citizenship education.

C. Frederick Risinger Mr. Risinger is Associate Director of the ERIC Clearinghouse for Social Studies/Social Science Education and Codirector of the Social Studies Development Center at Indiana University. Mr. Risinger has presented hundreds of workshops for social studies teachers throughout the country and has published widely. He has served as a consultant to several national educational projects. At present, Mr. Risinger is the Vice President of the National Council for the Social Studies.

Norris M. Sanders Norris Sanders is Professor Emeritus at the University of Wisconsin–Green Bay. He taught junior and senior high school for 20 years before teaching in the education department at UWGB. He has long been interested in promoting a variety of thinking skills by students and is the author of *Classroom Questions: What Kinds?* He is coauthor with Stephen Sanders of two social studies data-processing programs, published in 1989 by Great Lakes Software and distributed by Tom Snyder Productions.

Preface

Social studies teachers are well aware of fast technological changes taking place at a pace that boggles the mind. During this decade, computers and other technologies have become symbols of the Information Age and have forced us to develop new ways of learning and thinking. Both the production and flow of information influence our daily lives.

The Information Age has developed from an increase of new information and advances in technology that stores and transmits data. In the field of science alone, it is estimated that throughout the world at least two scientific articles are published for every minute of every day. In a lifetime, it is practically impossible for anyone to read all the articles produced in a single day. Yet we are judged by the information we have available to us and how we use that information in our personal and professional lives. The information we have shapes our values, actions, personalities, perspectives on the world, and the decisions we make.

This bulletin undertakes to provide readers with some ideas about ways social studies teachers may become effective teachers in an Information Age with its ever-increasing gap between what we understand and what we need to understand. Several chapters provide practical examples of ways teachers may help young people learn skills, content, and actions needed for effective citizenship behavior in the 1990s and beyond. These activities may be adapted for use at one or more grade levels. Other chapters describe resources currently available to help students and teachers gather information and move comfortably into the Information Age. Finally, still other chapters provide an overview of what is in social studies and challenge readers to extend their perspectives and thought beyond the here and now to the future.

This bulletin is intended to offer both a focus and a departure point for additional study and reflection on the effects of the Information Age upon us as citizens and teachers. Not all the current issues and emerging trends concerning classroom applications of the newer technologies have been addressed, and these must await a future NCSS bulletin.

The editors wish to thank the authors who shared their current thinking and prepared chapters for this bulletin. We also thank Salvatore Natoli, Director of Publications for the National Council for the Social Studies, who encouraged us to try new ideas in content and a new publication format. We express our appreciation to Anna Huven for original art work and to John DeBeck for word processing and formatting.

Green Bay and Madison, Wisconsin

March 1989

Margaret A. Laughlin
H. Michael Hartoonian
Norris M. Sanders

Chapter 1

Educating Students for an Information Age
Margaret A. Laughlin

"Where is the knowledge we have lost in information?
Where is the wisdom we have lost in knowledge?"
—T.S. Eliot, *Choruses from the Rock*

Introduction

This bulletin examines ways educators perceive the Information Age and react to it. Are we capitalizing on the increasing volume of data and information? Are we preparing students to be efficient producers and good citizens in a society that will be vastly different from the past and the present? Have we already become vulnerable to some of the errors identified by critics of information technology?

Wisdom
Knowledge
Information
Data

The words 'data' and 'information' are used in many ways. In social studies, we are accustomed to a hierarchy of facts, concepts, generalizations, and constructs. We now see increasing use of the hierarchy of data, information, knowledge, and wisdom. The term 'data' is used much more inclusively than 'facts'. Early information scientists were mathematicians or engineers. To them, data were the output of a sensor measuring the flow of fluid in a pipe or the changing temperature of coolant in an engine. Data are unprocessed and can be stored and communicated digitally. When data are patterned, they become information. Data from a sensor roughly fit the definition of 'facts', but in application by technicians they are phenomena that are unlikely to end up in an almanac or history book. The volume of data production is astronomically large. Most of the data serve a brief purpose to someone with highly specialized interests who then discards or stores the data on a tape to await some expiration date.

Constructs
Generalizations
Concepts
Facts

Data are so pervasive in our lives that we fail to realize their magnitude. Remote-sensing satellites orbit the planet 24 hours a day sending back data related to weather, land use, natural resources, crops, military deployment, and more. Law enforcement agencies manage millions of records on individuals. A grocer using bar code records has continuous information on available stock. What products need to be reordered? What stock is approaching its expiration date? Librarians track materials in circulation using data. Credit card companies collect data on billions of transactions. Governments are among the most active collectors of data. Think of the data collected and processed by the Internal Revenue Service. Virtually every agency of local, state, and national government is a heavy data user. Bankers and financiers collect and communicate great quantities of data.

Educating Students for an Information Age

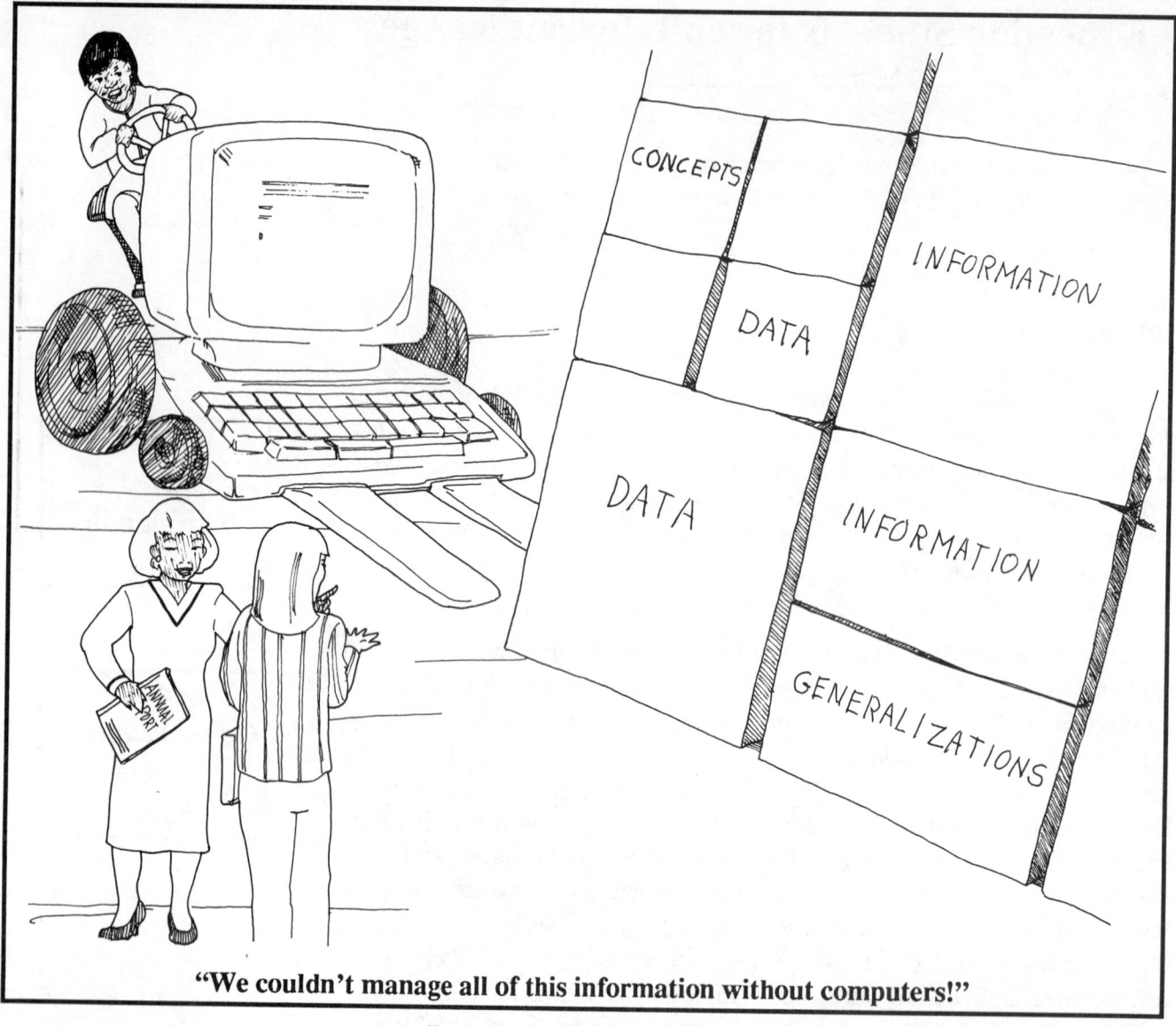

"We couldn't manage all of this information without computers!"

Both the words 'data' and 'facts' in everyday usage refer to verifiable observations or undisputed truths. However, they differ greatly in histories. We associate facts with scientific empiricism as it emerged in the 17th and 18th centuries. The current meaning of 'data' has developed since World War II and is closely associated with information theory and technology. Early pioneers in this new field were mathematicians like Norbert Wiener and Claude Shannon. Shannon developed a scientific definition of information and some laws of information that were extremely useful in developing new technology but were a long way from the concept of information used by educators and librarians.

In another strand of the story, someone in the U.S. Commerce Department noticed in the late 1950s that for the first time in our history there were more white-collar workers than blue-collar. Harvard sociologist Daniel Bell (1973) wrote a book on the "postindustrial society." Economist Fritz Machlup documented the growth of knowledge industries and in 1977 the Commerce Department published a nine-volume report entitled *The Information Economy* written mainly by economist Marc Uri Porat. None of these developments caused much general excitement until two books on the subject became best-sellers. One was *The Third Wave* in 1980, by Alvin Toffler, and the other was *Megatrends* in 1982, by John Naisbitt. Toffler described the "Infosphere" and Naisbitt wrote of the "global information economy."

Percentage of Households with Telephones in the United States
1920 35
1930 41
1940 37
1950 63
1960 78
1970 91
1980 96

More recently, the prediction of the demise of heavy industry in our nation has been declared premature. But industry is definitely changing as documented in Shoshana Zuboff's book, *In the Age of the Smart Machine* (1988). As a historian interested in the first industrial revolution, she studied ways the advent of machines changed the lives of working people. She began to realize that current changes in manufacturing were of the same magnitude as those that occurred a couple of centuries earlier. Zuboff spent prolonged periods visiting companies that were changed by information technology. The key was something she described as "informating." She studied the reactions of the workers as jobs changed and power shifted.

The information explosion is not confined to the Western world. W. Michael Blumenthal (1987/88, 535), Chief Executive Officer of the Unisys Corporation, told of a recent experience he had in the interior of China:

> A local farmer showed me his new television set on which he was just then watching Sam Donaldson, firing pointed questions at the president as he boarded his helicopter—but of course getting not much more than a cheerful grin and a wave in return, even in dubbed Chinese. The farmer thought it was great and I have not forgotten it since. When I was growing up in China, that illiterate peasant's horizon and knowledge about the outside world was limited by the distance he could walk or pedal his bicycle.

Fully informed citizens in an Information Age will need the ability to

- access data bases and information services
- understand sophisticated verbal, pictorial, and numeric data
- know the important published sources of information
- examine and process data from various perspectives
- apply the logic of social data analysis
- apply this information in daily life

Information Age Quotation
"Every historical period has its godword. There was an Age of Faith, an Age of Reason, an Age of Discovery. Our time has been nominated to be the Age of Information." (Roszak 1986, 19)

Educating Students for an Information Age

Not everyone welcomes the information explosion!

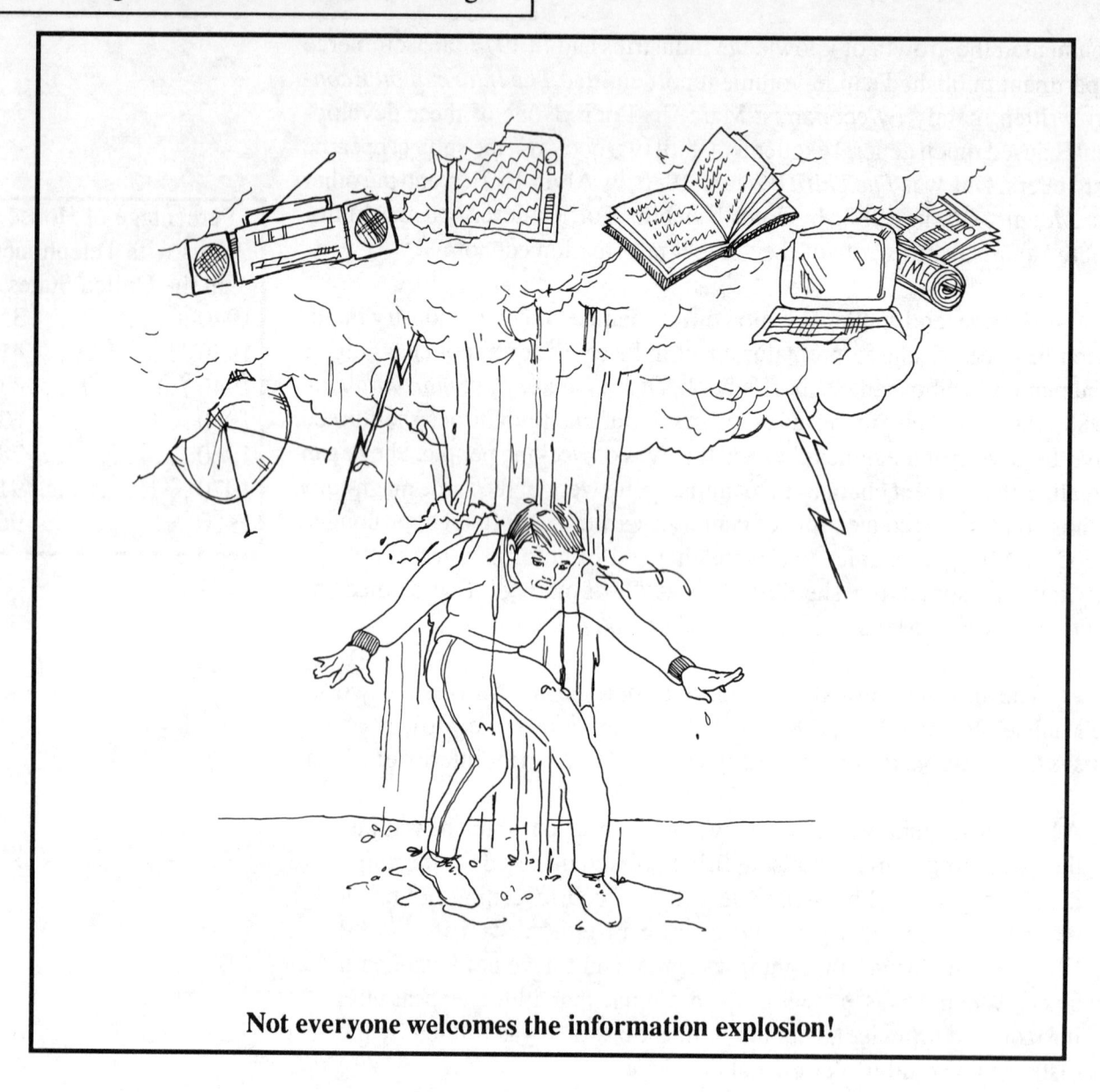

Critics of Information Technology

That not everyone welcomes the information explosion is evidenced by the following quotations:

> In spite of the abundance of information, or maybe partly because of it, the West has great difficulty in finding its bearings amid contemporary events. (Solzhenitsyn 1978, 39)

> Might it be the case that the retention of too much data—more than a single mind can judiciously deal with—compromises the quality of thought? I have surely come across a great many people who lose their intellectual way in a forest of facts. (Roszak 1986, 89)

The specter of "information overload" is real. More than 40,000 scientific articles are published annually. Specialists complain that they cannot read everything in their own narrow fields. Masses of information especially in statistical form are subject to misinterpretation, either unintentional or deliberate. A whole new generation of propaganda techniques has emerged with the advent of data and computers. Flawed opinion polling techniques are a prime example.

Number of Books Published in the United States
1919 8,594
1929 10,187
1939 10,640
1949 10,892
1959 14,876
1969 29,579
1980 42,377

Some fear that control of information will be used by a powerful few to exploit unskilled labor and minorities. The developing nations may be at a new kind of disadvantage in international affairs. On a personal level, the possibilities for invasion of privacy are enormous. It is frightening to think of the ways that we could be harmed by misuse of school records, credit accounts, tax files, medical records, traffic offenses, and dozens of similar files. This kind of information on everyone is stored on tapes and disks that can be called to a computer screen for purposes that may be good or evil.

The two pictures depict positive and negative judgments about the Information Age. In this bulletin, we find some justification for both views, but most authors tend to see the advantages of information technology. At the same time, we try to be alert to the abuses that worry the critics.

Social Studies in an Information Age

What is happening to social studies disciplines as we enter the Information Age? Changes in subject matter will obviously require teachers to master increasing amounts of social science content. The obvious fact is that each subject matter continues to produce additional information and knowledge. With new fields of knowledge emerging, knowledge is more fine-grained in one direction and more expansive in another. Alternative frames of reference and points of view abound in history, economics, and the rest of the social science disciplines. An increasing proportion of information is formulated numerically, and "social indicators" have emerged as one of many subdisciplines in the social sciences. This growing amount of knowledge is widely accessible via numerous indexes, interlibrary loans, on-line data bases, information centers, and the media industry. In an Information Age, teachers will become less the source of information and more brokers of information and facilitators of learning. The limiting factor is how much data and information persons will be able to assimilate and understand rather than how much is available. In spite of the information explosion, social studies textbooks have not become much fatter during the past 30 years and we still normally allot one to a student for each subject. This suggests that textbook authors digest increasing amounts of information and then prune and compact it tighter and tighter into textbooks. In protecting students from the flood of data, we may be doing them a disservice.

| Educating Students for an Information Age |

The Information Age invites us to jump disciplinary fences and develop broader perspectives by teaching with an interdisciplinary perspective, but school structure and organization and existing curriculum patterns often discourage such freedom, especially on the secondary level. Elementary and middle schools are organized in ways that make traversing traditional disciplinary boundaries easier. Learning environments can be decentralized and extended into homes, businesses, and the community. The problem we face is not that of an unwillingness to treat knowledge as a unity. Classification is essential to understanding, but classification distorts unities.

Subject matter rapidly becomes obsolete with new discoveries in science, innovations in technology, and refined research findings that help us understand and respond to what goes on in the world around us. For example, the half-life of a college degree in engineering is said to be slightly more than four years, which means that much of the current knowledge of an engineer will be largely obsolete within four or five years. The same seems true in the social sciences as well. No longer will a high school diploma or college degree be sufficient as adults have responsibilities to update knowledge, skills, and awareness of oneself and emerging policy issues.

Our current social studies curriculum embodies truth as scholars see it today, but today's knowledge is not the final version. Through social studies programs, students will be able to study problems of humankind and develop understandings about society shaped by microelectronic technology. In the year 2000, social studies educators may well laugh at the naïveté of a sizable portion of the content of current curriculum, but we do not now know which part will be considered humorous and in need of substantial revision.

If information grows so rapidly in volume, texture, and sophistication, how can teachers and students become and remain current? Can we continue to rely on new textbooks to bring teachers and students up to date? The obvious answer is no. Textbooks will serve a useful purpose but not carry the whole burden. The use of computers and other newer technologies will enable us to accumulate, store, locate, and manipulate data more readily and in vastly more efficient ways than in the past. With much of the world's information readily available at our fingertips, it is important that social studies educators prepare young people for their roles and responsibilities as enlightened citizens in the 21st century.

This NCSS bulletin seeks to address these concerns and encourages social studies educators to grapple intellectually with these issues and consider ways to help young people use data in their roles as citizens, producers, consumers, family members, and so on. We aim at finding an equitable balance between theory and practice. We do not approach curriculum change as if starting with a clean slate. There are the common grade level assignments of major content in the K–12 social studies curriculum and the related concepts, generalizations, and skills drawn from the social sciences and related disciplines. The superstructure of state mandates, class schedules, lesson plans, class management details, textbooks, accountability measures, and limited budgets is in place. The question is, What can we do to bring about significant progress?

An Overview

This publication offers several perspectives about what it means to be an active participant in the Information Age. The authors of chapters 2 through 5 suggest ways teachers can work with students at several grade levels or grade-level clusters to gather data, make sense of the data, and use the data in making personal decisions. For example, Messick and Chapin note that social information abounds in classroom experiences and suggest several valuable learning activities that young people can use to gather data and apply them to their daily lives. They also suggest examples of computer programs that teachers may find useful for students as they practice decision-making skills.

Koch and Remy recognize the complexity of data and offer practical suggestions for defining, researching, and dissecting social issues. Koch offers a skills model to help young people understand data and provides examples of questions teachers need to ask of themselves as students plan to gather or generate data, and interpret and use data in making a variety of personal and public decisions. Questions are also suggested for student use as well. Remy suggests ways students can discuss social issues topics that require them to engage in decision-making processes on the basis of conflicting but often valid information. He offers a decision-making tree as a model in which students need to consider the probable positive and negative consequences of a given decision. Students' use of the two models suggested by Koch and Remy has implications and value not only for social studies education but for other curriculum content areas as well.

Using census data, Dailey and Engelhardt describe the United States Census Bureau Educational Project in which teachers assist students in using information generated by the Census Bureau to improve their understanding of social, political, and economic phenomena in our nation. Incidentally, the Census Bureau is a governmental agency with vast amounts of information that are readily available for use in schools.

The next part of the bulletin presents three chapters dealing with notions and concepts related to social mathematics. As more and more information is formulated numerically, teachers and students ought to know about quantitative concepts that are useful in social analysis. Hartoonian provides an excellent overview of the importance of social mathematics and suggests examples at several grade levels of how social mathematics concepts and skills can be included in social studies instruction and in the social studies curriculum. Most of the mathematics skills have been introduced to students by the 6th grade. Lengel and Sanders recommend several tools and ideas for learning activities on computers that social studies educators can use to help young people develop social mathematics competencies and use quantitative social data. While recognizing the potential of the computer to deal with an accelerated flow of information and knowledge, both Lengel and Sanders emphasize traditional roles for teachers.

The next two chapters (9 and 10) describe sources of information useful for social studies educators in gathering and interpretating data. Callison describes five teaching methodologies for social studies teachers that extend beyond the confines of the traditional social studies textbook. In addition, Callison discusses some of the new information technologies now available in many schools for student and faculty use. Risinger discusses the importance for social studies teachers of the Educational Resources Information Center (ERIC) as a source of information on such matters as current trends in social studies, sample curriculum guides, examples of instructional units and lessons, and reports from various sources. Risinger describes current and future plans for ERIC.

Moseley, in a fictitious interview, offers the perspective of an educational publisher trying to determine what ought to be included and excluded from books, grappling with various societal and educational issues, and trying to meet the needs of educators and students and the expectations of the larger community. He asks important questions for which answers can at best be only tentative. Although he admonishes educators for not using the expertise of textbook developers in curriculum building, he also recounts economic and political reasons why textbook publishers find it difficult to be more assertive in educational innovation.

Finally, the concluding chapter brings together key ideas about the Information Age and poses important questions and issues that require further attention. The Information Age is new and revolutionary. Where it will lead is uncertain. What is certain is that we need to be ready to respond to further changes as we exercise our citizenship responsibilities.

References

Bell, D. *The Coming of Post Industrial Society*. New York: Basic Books, 1973.

Blumenthal, W.M. "The World Economy and Technological Change." *Foreign Affairs* 66, no. 3 (1987/88): 529–50.

Machlup, F. *The Production and Distribution of Knowledge in the United States*. Princeton, New Jersey: Princeton University Press, 1962.

Naisbitt, J. *Megatrends*. New York: Warner Books, 1982.

Porat, M. *The Information Economy*. Washington, D.C.: U.S. Department of Commerce, 1977.

Roszak, T. *The Cult of Information*. New York. Pantheon Books, 1986.

Solzhenitsyn, A. *A World Split Apart*. New York: Harper and Row, 1978.

Toffler, A. *The Third Wave*. New York: Random House, 1980.

Zuboff, S. *In the Age of the Smart Machine*. New York: Basic Books, 1988.

Information Age Quotation

"We are at the dawn of the era of the smart machine—an 'information' age that will change forever the way an entire nation works, plays, travels, and even thinks. Just as the industrial revolution expanded the strength of man's muscles and the reach of his hand, so the smart-machine revolution will magnify the power of his brain. But unlike the industrial revolution, which depended on finite resources such as iron and oil, the new information age will be fired by a seemingly limitless resource—the inexhaustible supply of knowledge itself." —"Machines That Think," *Newsweek*, June 30, 1980, 50.

Information Age Quotation

"Data, data, everywhere, but not a thought to think." —Jesse H. Shea, quoted by Roszak 1986, 37.

Information Age Quotations

A small group of scholars dispute the 'postindustrial' and 'information' society labels, arguing that characteristics of capitalism continue to dominate society.... We propose a third interpretation of the origins of the information society, in which we describe a social structure that is capitalistic and industrial, but distinctly oriented to information. We see the information phenomena as historically significant, but reject the notion that the patterns of an information society represent a break from those of the industrial period. Instead, we propose that the information phenomena reflect the continuing evolution of industrial capitalism, which has resulted in an information-oriented society in the United States. —Jorge Reina Schement and Leah A. Lievrouw, "A Third Vision: Capitalism and the Industrial Origins of the Information Society," *Competing Visions, Complex Realities: Social Aspects of an Information Society* (Norwood, New Jersey: Ablex Publishing Corporation, 1987), 38.

In an information-rich polity, the very definition of control changes. Very large numbers of people empowered by knowledge—coming together in parties, unions, factions, lobbies, interest groups, neighborhoods, families, and hundreds of other structures—assert the right or feel the obligation to make policy.

Decision making proceeds not by the flow of recommendations up and orders down, but by the development of a shared sense of direction.... Not command and control, but conferring and networking become the mandatory mode for getting things done.... More participatory decision making implies a need for much information, widely dispersed and much feedback, seriously attended. —Harlan Cleveland, "The Twilight of Hierarchy: Speculations on the Global Information Society," in *Information Technologies and Social Transformation*, ed. Bruce R. Guile (Washington, D.C.: National Academy Press, 1985), 62.

Just as Marshall McLuhan's fish could not perceive water, so we are largely unaware of information, the medium in which we work, draw sustenance, and swim through life. As living beings we are constantly processing information.... Within this information context, the common work of education can be described as decision making.... The nature of the fundamental work of education, therefore, is responsive situational decision making. This view is supported by research that suggests that effective teachers, principals, and superintendents function much as ships' captains do—staying constantly alert to the unanticipated; monitoring their expectations for the unexpected; and making progress by a series of small decisions, each based on the previous ones. —Lewis A. Rhodes, "We Have Met the System—And It Is Us," *Phi Delta Kappan*, September 1988, 29.

Chapter 2

Using Data in Elementary Social Studies Programs

Rosemary G. Messick and
June R. Chapin

Students, as active learners, are busily engaged in perceiving and interpreting data, which leads to their construction and reconstruction of social reality. Whether this social reality includes the knowledge and skills of civic decision making depends on the kinds of experiences children have. For young children, school is the first civic arena. Both intentional and unintended experiences are crucial to their development as rational, civically conscious problem solvers.

> *For young children, school is the first civic arena.*

Teachers have two broad, related guidelines to follow in facilitating children's development of social reality. The first is to recognize the cognitive, psychological, and social characteristics that impinge on children's ability to relate to data. The second is to develop the art of selecting and arranging appropriate settings in which children become ever more conscious of their use and creation of data. These acts lend more or less power to their thinking.

Fitting the Task to the Child

Recognizing these developmental contingencies is the first step for structuring appropriate experiences in civic decision making. The second step is determining how to structure the curriculum to focus on civic decision making. Two layers of the curriculum need to be considered in this step. The most basic layer is the civic culture of the classroom society. The topics we choose to study constitute the second layer. Let us look briefly at developmental contingencies that guide our curriculum thinking and at two layers of curriculum organization: the civic culture of the classroom and topics of study.

Characteristics of Young Children. The developmental tasks typical for primary grade children (K–4) must guide the structuring of situations that lead to data generation, interpretation, and decision making. Young children are engaged in expanding their egocentric view of the world. They learn, often reluctantly, to take the perspectives of other persons. In the process of *decentering,* they perceive that one person can incorporate several roles. They begin to group or classify phenomena by characteristics, e.g., size, shape, or age. Psychologically, they are less introspective and more able at physical than verbal expression of feelings. For children of this age, competition and group work are new and often stultifying. They are only beginning to become interested in the product as well as the process of their learning.

Using Data in Elementary Social Studies Programs

Children in the intermediate grades (5–8) are more able to deal cognitively with what is unfamiliar than children in primary grades. They can see themselves in the context of time as well as space. Psychologically, most middle graders enjoy individual challenges and team activities. They spend extended periods working on projects and making products. Socially, middle-grade children are keenly aware of fairness and enforced rules. They assume reciprocity in friendship and see that their acts have social consequences.

Classroom Culture. Living and working together in a classroom setting can become an experience in civic decision making. The classroom that reflects habits of democratic ideals of individual rights and concomitant responsibilities, equality of opportunity, due process, and consent of the governed in the conduct of daily living helps teach young children these ideals. Too often, however, classroom management "systems" deny children opportunities to observe their own and others' behavior and make conclusions or rules about how good relations and learning can best be promoted. Finding ways to infuse classroom management with opportunities for children to participate meaningfully requires that teachers think about the larger goal of civic education. Asking first graders, for example, to vote on an issue of classroom procedure such as lining up to go out for recess or electing the "citizen of the week" may not be meaningful to the children or useful to classroom efficiency as a decision-making exercise. On the other hand, discussing the good examples of cleaning up before leaving for recess and keeping individual check-off charts that give access to the class "good citizenship club" are positive and developmentally meaningful to young children. Classroom routines and information sharing based on visual representations of "class data" instruct young children about the habit of measuring and counting representations of the real world. Ongoing activities that chart classroom events such as losing teeth, having birthdays, reading books, growing seeds, and feeding animals provide ways of representing events that lend children a heightened sense of history and time. Compiling an ongoing classroom diary, journal, or time line that stretches around the classroom walls allows young children to look back at their shared yesterdays and connect them to today's events. Rather than using data to make group decisions, as is appropriate for older students, the focus for young children is on using data that assists them individually to construct and reconstruct their worlds.

> *Students need to tackle real issues and make real decisions that are carried out.*

Although using data to make group decisions is not necessarily part of young children's repertoire, middle graders take delight in it. Scheduled times for student-led class meetings reinforce the meaningfulness of the decision-making process. If the power of class meetings as an exercise in decision making is to be realized, students need to tackle issues close to their lives and make real decisions to carry out. Teachers can promote these activities by the questions and problems they pose about classroom procedures for children to investigate. Organizing teams to collect data, for example, on what happens to the playground equipment after recess or how long it takes to handle announcements or check papers will involve coaching children on how to record what they count, time, or observe. Once data from a series of events or days are collected and organized, children have some tangible information to reflect upon. They can discuss the reliability of the data, and suggest ways to change or improve the situation based on reasons or criteria for the change. If they record these reasons, the new routine can be evaluated to see whether it does respond to the class-created criteria or standards.

Topics for Study

Finding the fit between the developmental stages and topics of study that involve the civic decision-making cycle continues to be a challenge. Finding avenues that open personal engagement with larger issues to children is essential for capturing interest. Extending the possibility through the accumulation of data about the issue and viewing the issue from more than one perspective is the instructional obligation.

Conventional wisdom confines primary-grade children to topics consistent with the tangibles of their daily lives. Thus analyzing how the work of the world gets done begins with the family unit and moves on to the school and neighborhood. Changes in the context of young children's daily lives suggest that we need to see these conventional topics in a global context. Veteran kindergarten teacher Barbara Schubert's experience illustrates the significance of contextual change. Schubert incorporated the use of a globe with toy sharing. Whenever a kindergartner brought a toy to sharing time, Schubert helped the child find out where the toy had been manufactured. Red adhesive dots were placed on the globe to identify the toy's point of origin. Over time the stickers began to accumulate in certain areas—Taiwan, Hong Kong, and Japan. Schubert led the class to talk about trade. They became curious about the sources of their clothing and food and about what their local area produced for the rest of the world. She was amazed that the children were persistent in their interest and able to verbalize thoughts about such abstract and wide-ranging topics. Children brought their parents into the classroom to show them the globe and were able to tell them about the location of the dots as well as what they meant. The topic was informal and ongoing and, as Schubert discovered, developmentally appropriate. In part, this topic was possible to teach because of changes in children's lives caused by expanded world trade, television, family mobility, and immigration. Of equal importance, we would argue, to unlocking this kind of a topic for young children was the impetus Schubert used: Toys are personal and prized. (Note: Barbara

Schubert formerly taught at Blackford School in Campbell Union School District, Campbell, California. She is currently Curriculum Coordinator with the Santa Clara County Office of Education, San Jose, California.)

Issue-oriented topics that concern natural resources can engage middle-grade students. Their almost universal love of animals makes research on endangered species an attractive theme upon which to build integrated science and social science experiences. Data collection on the habitats, habits, population, reasons for decline, and measures to protect and rescue individual species is an essential beginning to exploring what can and should be done to maintain the world's biological variability. Other topical possibilities that could also incorporate a complex cycle of civic decision making are local and regional land use and planning.

Most textbooks do not, indeed could not, provide the amount and variety of data required to entertain issue-oriented topics.

Organizing an issue-oriented unit assumes that elements of history and geography will be naturally infused into the research. For example, to understand the current transportation in a given locale, it is important to uncover reasons for building or pulling out rail or trolley lines or constructing canals and locks. Were there spring floods and summer drought seasons to overcome? Did the rivers run contrary to where goods needed to go? Did private individuals or public monies build the lines? Did freeways connect new population centers or follow old routes? Which came first, roads or population centers? Most textbooks do not, indeed could not, provide the amount and variety of data required to entertain issue-oriented topics. To engage students in research of this sort, teachers need to prepare an array of source materials. To undertake topics that involve students in the complete cycle of civic decision making requires team efforts and locally oriented curriculum work undertaken over time.

Data-Generating Strategies

Elements of the processes and skills involved in civic decision making can be incorporated in all social studies topics. Reviewing some of the data-generating strategies highlights several possibilities and materials.

Historical Newspapers, Diaries, and Letters. Organizing a set of locally and regionally pertinent copies of historical newspapers for distribution to teachers facilitates relating the past to the present. All newspapers keep archives. Most would gladly contribute a sample that focused on reproducing the local version of major events such as the explosion of the atomic bomb or that included a sample copy of the newspaper from each decade since publication began. The comparisons that could be made depend on the topic under study, but could range from prices of items on sale advertised at local retail outlets to styles of dress and major public policy issues.

Any historical topic is enriched by reading diaries and letters written by people of the period. Excerpts from diaries that are related to issues or events can bring data about a period to life for children. Two examples that could enrich the human side of national issues are the collection of famous speeches by noted Indian chieftains: *Indian Oratory* (Vanderwerth 1971) and first-person narratives of escapes to freedom in the North in *The Underground Railroad* (Blockson 1987).

More recent events such as the Vietnam War or the effects of the Peace Corps can be illuminated by family letters. Middle-grade students should be alerted to asking parents and grandparents about letters saved from wartime or immigration experiences. Reading such letters opens up the complexity of issues as well as the reality of daily living in the past and their families' connection to it.

Oral History. Collecting oral histories can be a powerful means of sensitizing children to the importance of process in reconstructing the past. Interviewing senior citizens and grandparents in their communities gives children greater appreciation of the worth of seniors and can strengthen the bonds between the generations.

A fertile initial oral history topic is interviewing senior citizens about what elementary school was like when they attended. Children are fascinated by knowledge about their grade level. Questions about what subjects were taught, number of hours in school, games played, transportation to school, and what discipline the teacher used have high interest.

Questions for the interview should be short and simple. They need to practice the etiquette of asking their respondents' permission to use their information for a class project. Each student needs to prepare a written copy of the questions. Before going to their sources, children need to practice interview techniques in class. They should anticipate how they will record answers to their questions. They need practice in note-taking if that is the mode of collection chosen. If they plan to tape the interview, they need to practice taking notes from the tape.

Data from oral interviews are excellent vehicles for practicing the historian's craft. Students can examine whether respondents embellished the truth. Did they really walk two miles to school in three feet of snow? Does the person only remember the pleasant things about school? Students need to discuss what causes people to have selective memories about past events. By comparing different interviews on the same topic, students can plot areas of agreement about what life was like in elementary school. To support their hunches about these similarities and differences, they should go back to their data and compare the ages of their respondents or the places they went to school. For further corroboration, teachers can call upon the resources of the local historical society. Oral history projects move students from the passive role of reading about history to an active role of collecting and analyzing data about the past.

> *If the content inspiring data generation is linked to children's interests, they will enjoy the process.*

Time-Lapse Map Study. Using a series of maps or pictures that portray local and regional development over time helps students make spatial connections to the past. To make a visual composite of city or regional growth, students can color-code a current map according to periods portrayed on the various historical maps of the same area. Tracing names of neighborhoods, streets, and other prominent points of interest over time can uncover the changes in ethnic or tribal settlement patterns.

Students can trace the study of growth, transportation, and trade through a series of historical maps. Frequently, highways were built over native trails. Settlements often grew or stopped growing depending upon whether a railroad, canal, or paved road was built nearby. Middle-grade students can connect products to kinds of transportation. For example, mining centers are linked to manufacturing centers by rail or waterways. Historical map series show that cities and agriculture in the Southwest grew with the development of reservoir and canal systems.

Using a series of historical maps can be overwhelming to middle grade children. They need to narrow the data array and focus on telling the story of just one name, trail, river, or block on the various maps. They will find that to confirm guesses about their topic, they need to locate other resources. Although maps alone do not tell all the details students need to flesh out the story of their place, they are a good beginning.

> *The primacy of group discussion throughout the data-gathering process is essential.*

Several microcomputer programs on mapping are now available for younger children (*Sticky Bear Town Builder*, 1985; "City Blocks" in *Microzine*, 1987). The intent of the programs is exploratory. Children may, as with building blocks or a collection of cardboard containers, move about graphics of streets, buildings, trees, and vehicles on the monitor screen to build their versions of communities. The payoffs of these programs come with the spatial reconstructing, tactile experiences, and discussing with computer partners what the programs represent. Teachers with printers can further enhance the children's interaction with data by having them tell how people would have places to play, be protected from the traffic, or get their food and other needs met using their printed "maps."

Data Bases. Included in all the strategies for generating data, of course, are data bases. The hypothesis-testing kinds of thinking that can be promoted with data bases make them absolute musts for issue-oriented topics that require comparison and analysis. Traditionally, teachers have organized parallel groups to gather data and fill in the cells of a wall-sized retrieval chart. Horizontally, the cells typically listed common cultural characteristics such as food sources, shelter type, religious beliefs, clothing styles, recreation, family education, profession, location, contributions, and famous quotations. Vertically, the group topics such as Native American groups or famous people of the Revolutionary War were listed. After the class heard general group presentations, they could compare and contrast the groups and generalize about the broader topic based on the data contained in the chart constructed by the class group study.

Now electronic retrieval charts such as *Bank Street School Filer* (Pleasantville, New York: Sunburst, 1986) provide a technologically assisted way to stimulate drawing comparisons and testing hypotheses. Continuing to input classroom data gives repeated opportunity to interact with the mechanics and play with the power of rearranging the data. Data collections can be built on topics tailored to the interests of students: books read by individuals, movies seen, personal surveys of experiences, preferences in food, music, television shows, tracking weather and climate in world cities from daily newspapers, team and individual sports statistics, and individual daily calorie intake. The personal nature of the data and the electronic ability to display rearrangements of it can encourage students to call up comparisons.

> *The stages of problem solving... need to be incorporated into any data-gathering strategy and explicitly highlighted.*

More premade data base microcomputer programs are coming onto the market. Many require students to use them as electronic references. For example, *pfs: U.S. History Data Bases* (1985) comes with teacher instructions to get students started in posing questions that probe and *re*-sort data according to different categories. From the file on presidents, students can check their guesses from the trivial—that all bachelor presidents were Republicans—to the slightly more significant—that almost all presidents come from east of the Mississippi River.

Some premade data bases are embedded in simulation-type formats. *The Oregon Trail* (1985) is probably the one known best. Students are placed in roles that require decision making based on data as the trip from Missouri to Oregon unfolds. The *Carmen Sandiego* (1985) series has forced more students to become familiar with the *World Almanac* than generations of teachers combined! Geographical data and note-taking must be used successfully to trace the elusive Carmen. Other programs that involve the use of data are available. For example, *The Sea Voyagers* (1985) provides students a biographical profile of explorers from 1400 to 1800 and then provides data on maps, charts, models, graphs, tables, pictures, and cartoons that students must interpret to "play the game." Such programs can be used to link the traditionally reading-based social studies curriculum to an interactive setting that gives students practice in using data to make decisions.

Summary

What general guidelines for the elementary teacher emerge from the several data-generation strategies outlined in this chapter? First, skills should not be taught in isolation from interesting and relevant content. This means that the development of data-generation skills cannot be separated from either the content or the values that govern their use. If the content inspiring data generation is linked to children's interests, they will enjoy the process. Second, the stages of problem solving—identifying a problem, formulating a tentative hypothesis, data gathering, and accepting or rejecting the original hypothesis—need to be incorporated into any data-gathering strategy and explicitly highlighted. Third, the primacy of group discussion throughout the data-gathering process is essential. Students should constantly be working in small groups and brought back to the whole group when they are engaged in understanding the meaning of the processes and the data. When the give-and-take of group discussion is based on data gathered about a topic of student concern, we can be assured that the thinking skills necessary for personal competency and effective citizenship are being developed.

References

Bank Street School Filer. Pleasantville, New York: Sunburst, 1986.

Blockson, C. *The Underground Railroad*. Englewood Cliffs, New Jersey: Prentice-Hall, 1987.

Carmen Sandiego. San Rafael, California: Broderbund, 1985.

"City Blocks," in *Microzine*. Jefferson City, Missouri: Scholastic, 1987.

Diem, R.C. *Computers in the Classroom*. How-to-Do-It Series 2, No. 4, Washington, D.C.: National Council for the Social Studies, 1981.

The Oregon Trail. St. Paul, Minnesota: Minnesota Educational Computer Consortium, 1985.

pfs: U.S. History Data Bases. Jefferson City, Missouri: Scholastic, 1985.

The Sea Voyagers. Greenwich, Connecticut: CBA, 1985.

Sticky Bear Town Builder. Columbus, Ohio: Weekly Reader Family Software, 1985.

Truett, C. "The Search for Quality Microprograms: Software and Review Sources." *School Library Journal* (January 1984): 35–37.

Vanderwerth, W.C. *Indian Oratory*. Norman, Oklahoma: University of Oklahoma Press, 1971.

White, C.S., and A.D. Glenn. "Computers in the Curriculum: Social Studies." *Electronic Learning* (September 1984): 54–64.

Strategic Thinking in the Social Studies
Kathryn A. Koch

For students to gather, record, understand, and use data independently in the social studies, they need to *analyze* the task before them and *plan* to succeed by thinking about their purpose, setting reasonable goals, and choosing appropriate learning strategies. Students need to *monitor* and *regulate* how well they gather, record, understand, and use data. They should think while completing the task and change goals and strategies, as necessary, to be able to understand, remember, and use information attained. Such students are strategic thinkers because they are aware of and control their use of skills and strategies (Cook 1986; Jones, Palincsar, Ogle, and Carr 1987; Paris, Lipson, and Wixson 1983).

> *Students need to monitor and regulate how well they gather, record, understand, and use data.*

The phases of the social studies data process are illustrated in Figure 1. A pie diagram is used for three reasons. First, it can be used in explaining the data process to students. Second, no sequence for the phases is implied, inasmuch as no single order is the correct one and some phases often need to be used several times in the process. For example, possible sequences include selecting the topic, formulating questions, gathering data, selecting questions, gathering additional data, recording data, understanding data, and reporting information; or selecting the topic, selecting questions, gathering data, understanding information, and using information.

Figure 1.

[Pie diagram with center "UNDERSTAND DATA" surrounded by: Select Topic, Formulate Questions, Select Questions, Gather Data, Record Data, Report Information, Use Information]

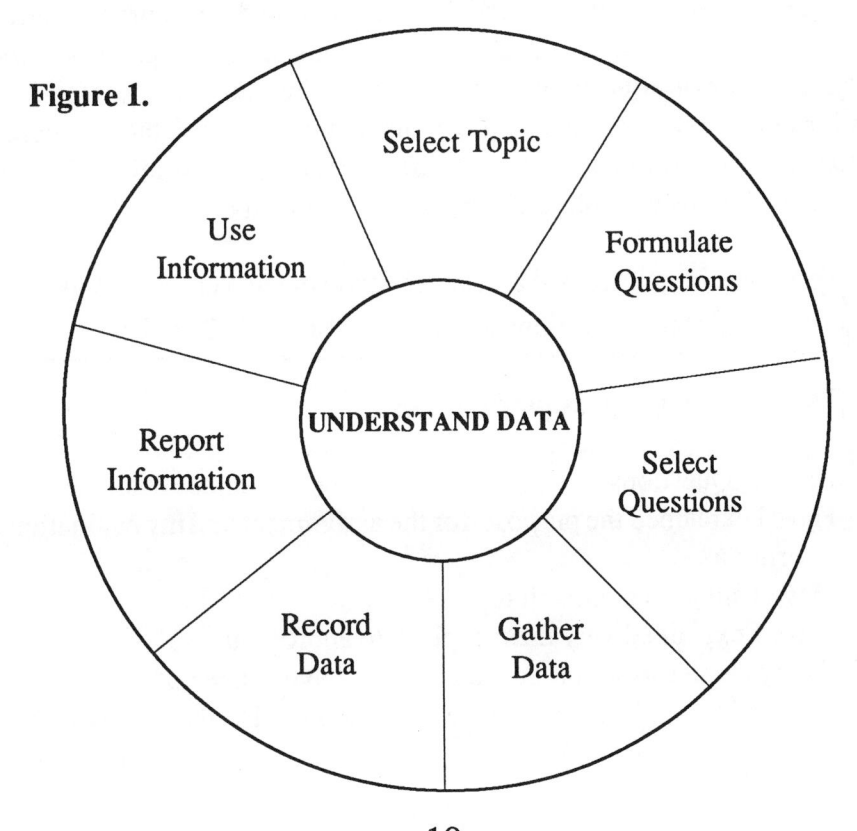

A pie diagram also allows teachers to demonstrate that students' purposes and assignments influence the emphasis placed on each phase. For example, reporting the information to others might be more important at one time than at another. By making that piece of the diagram larger and decreasing or even eliminating a phase, teachers can demonstrate where they want students to concentrate their efforts.

For students to be strategic thinkers, they need to understand the purposes and strategies of each phase of the social studies data process. An elaboration of the phases in a likely sequence follows.

> *For students to be strategic thinkers, they need to understand the purposes and strategies of each phase of the social studies data process.*

Topic and Question Selection

There are many social studies topics that students may have questions about. Devine (1987, 205) suggests the following guidelines for choosing topics:

> Students must select one that (1) they are personally curious about, (2) they are qualified by age and experience to handle, and (3) they can deal with in the time limitations set by the course and teacher. Two other considerations need to be examined by the class as a whole before students make final choices: Are library [and other] resources available in this subject? Is the question open to investigation?

The use of data in the social studies requires worthwhile questions. These general and specific questions can be found in course materials, formulated by teachers, or suggested by students. The data process is most effective when many questions are formulated. This allows students to delete questions that no longer interest them, that are irrelevant to the assignment, and that are inappropriate because of time or material constraints. They will still have questions to explore if they begin with many.

Examples of questions that teachers and students can use to guide the selection of topics and questions are listed in Tables 1, 2, and 3.

Table 1. Guide for Topic Selection

Teacher Questions
Have I explained the purpose for the assignment and my evaluation criteria?
Have I suggested enough topics?
Have I explained why these topics are appropriate?
Are resources available for the topics I have suggested?
Should I let students choose their own topics? Do they know how?

(continued)

Table 1. Guide for Topic Selection (continued)
Should I check students' topics before they begin to formulate questions?

Student Questions
What am I interested in learning more about?
Why does this topic interest me?
Will the teacher accept this topic for the assignment?
If I choose this topic, will I be able to gather relevant data? Are there enough appropriate materials? Do I have enough time?

Table 2. Guide for Question Formulation

Teacher Questions
Are there questions in our text or other instructional materials that can be used?
Should I suggest questions that I believe are worthwhile?
Have I taught students how to compose their own questions?
Should they suggest their own?
Do students know enough about the topic to formulate their own questions?
Should I check the students' progress? How?

Student Questions
What do I want to know about this topic?
What questions can be asked about my topic?
Have I started questions with *what, who, when, where, why, how, should, could, would,* and *are?*
Have I used important verbs such as *compare, define, describe, explain, identify, name,* and *predict* in my questions?
Are my questions appropriate for the assignment?
Do I have enough questions?

Table 3. Guide for Question Selection

Teacher Questions
Have I reminded students of the assignment's purpose(s) so they will choose the most appropriate questions?
Should I assign certain questions to specific students?
Should I determine whether students' questions are appropriate, specific, and understandable before they begin to gather data?

(continued)

Table 3. Guide for Question Selection (continued)

Student Questions
Which questions do I most want to answer? Why?
Should I add or revise any questions?
Are the questions appropriate for the assignment?
Do I understand the questions?
Will I be able to answer my question? Do I have the necessary reading, writing, and computation skills?
Will I be able to find answers in the time available?

Gathering Data

Students begin gathering data during and after the topic and questions are chosen. They need to decide which primary or secondary sources to use. Primary data can be collected by interviewing people, conducting polls, and designing activities that result in new data. Data gathered and organized by others can be found in a variety of secondary (or archival) sources. For example, textbooks, reference books, library books, magazines, newspapers, documents, data bases, maps, films, television shows, and lectures may all contain information relevant to students' topic and questions.

If students will be collecting data from graphs, tables, or maps, it is important to teach them how to read them. Students should understand the specific purposes of different graphs. Picture graphs use pictures to express quantities, bar graphs compare quantities using horizontal or vertical bars, pie graphs show how parts are related to the whole, and line graphs show changes over time. Students should also be taught to use tables for listing facts in an organized way.

Students can observe the following steps when reading various graphs (Burns, Roe, and Ross 1988; Dechant 1982):
 1. Read the title to learn the purpose of the graph.
 2. Discover what is being compared.
 3. Interpret the legend or the meaning of the horizontal and vertical axes.
 4. Draw conclusions from the data provided.

These steps work when students need to gather data from tables (Burns, Roe, and Ross 1988; Dechant 1982):
 1. Read the title to learn the purpose of the table.
 2. Read the column headings.
 3. Read the details from the far left column.
 4. Locate the column and row intersection that contains the relevant data.

Data will frequently be gathered from one of the major map types: landform, elevation, climate, vegetation and water features, economic, population, and political. As with graphs and tables, students need to understand the purposes of these different maps. According to Summers (1965), students should be aware of these map elements: title, legend, direction, distance scale, and the location grid system.

Examples of questions to guide the data-gathering process are listed in Table 4.

Table 4. Guide for Gathering Data

Teacher Questions
- Have I taught specific information about primary data-collection methods?
- Have I taught students how to find relevant secondary sources?
- To what extent should I help students find relevant sources?
- Have I taught specific aspects of relevant reading, listening, writing, and studying skills so students can use secondary sources independently?
- Do students understand how to use graphs, tables, and maps?
- Should I check students' progress? How?

Student Questions
- Should I gather data from primary sources?
- Which library, class, and community sources might contain relevant data?
- Have I gathered data from a variety of sources?
- Are the data relevant to my questions?
- Have I gathered enough data?
- Do I need to revise, delete, or add questions in light of what I have gathered?
- Do I understand the data?

Recording Data

Students should usually begin recording as they collect data since it is often during this phase that they will determine whether they have enough data. In selecting the recording system, students should keep in mind both the questions and the type of data to be collected. It may be appropriate to take notes in an outline or informal phrase format. The data might be displayed in a picture, bar, pie, or line graph, a table, diagram, or map. It might be necessary to begin with notes and then to decide how to summarize the data.

Table 5 contains sample questions to guide the data-recording process.

Table 5. Guide for Recording Data

Teacher Questions
Have I taught specific aspects of several recording methods (e.g., outlining, semantic mapping, graphing, note cards)?
Have I taught students how to reference their data?
Have I taught students how to organize their records?
Should I check students' progress? How?

Student Questions
Is my recording system appropriate for the data and questions?
Will I be able to answer my questions?
Should I gather additional data?
Are my records complete?
Are my records organized?
Should I delete or add questions in light of what I am recording?
Do I understand the data?

Understanding Data

Understanding needs to be a goal throughout the data process. Therefore, it is the center of the pie diagram in Figure 1. For example, students need to gather and record data for immediate and long-term understanding so they can use the information in the future. They need to concentrate on what the data mean and not just the mechanics of gathering and recording. Students should be taught how to think about the data in light of their questions. If the data are not understood, students can ask additional questions, gather additional data, record differently, or study the data further.

Students need to concentrate on what the data mean and not just the mechanics of gathering and recording.

The understanding-data phase can be guided by the sample questions in Table 6.

Table 6. Guide for Understanding Data

Teacher Questions
Have I taught students how to study and think about data in light of their questions?
Have I taught students how to evaluate the quality of their understanding?

(continued)

Table 5. Guide for Understanding Data (continued)

Have I taught students what to do when data are confusing or incomplete?
Should I check the students' progress? How?

Student Questions
Do I understand the data well enough to answer my question?
Should I study the data further?
Do I need to gather new data to confirm the answers or complete my understanding?
Would recording and organizing the data in new ways change the answers?
Are my answers clearly supported by my data?
Am I surprised by any answers?
What answers interest me the most?
Are there new questions that need to be asked?

Reporting and Using Information

If students need to report their answer to others, they should decide how best to do this. Decisions about when and how to use the information in the future also need to be made. One important use of information is for formulating new questions. In this way, the data process never ends but is ongoing.

Questions to guide these processes are listed in Tables 7 and 8.

Table 7. Guide for Reporting Information

Teacher Questions
　Have I taught specific aspects of several reporting methods (e.g., written formats, visual displays, oral presentations)?
　Should I let students choose their own reporting method?
　Have I reminded students how I will evaluate this assignment?
　Should I check students' progress? How?

Student Questions
　Do I understand the information well enough to explain it to someone else?
　Who might be interested in the information?
　Should I report all or part of the information?
　What written, visual, or oral presentations are appropriate for explaining the information to others? Is one format better than the others?　　　　　　　　　　　(continued)

Table 7. Guide for Reporting Information (continued)

Do I have the necessary skills to report the information with my chosen method?

Have I chosen the most appropriate format and information in the assignment?

Table 8. Guide for Using Information

Teacher Questions

Have I taught students why it is beneficial to use new information in the future?

Have I taught students how to use information in the future? Will they be able to see relationships among topics so as to be able to use relevant information?

To what extent should I help students use information with other course topics or curriculum areas?

Have I reminded students how I will evaluate this assignment?

Should I check students' progress? How?

Student Questions

How can I use this information in the future?

To what course topics is my information related?

Is my information related to other courses?

Does the information suggest new questions I would like answered?

Am I using the information in appropriate ways for the assignment?

Data Strategies

Students should learn various strategies so they can gather, record, understand, and use data successfully and independently. Teachers can select strategies that are appropriate for their goals and the demands of their curriculum, textbooks, and assignments. Once the data strategies are chosen, these guidelines are useful in increasing students' abilities to analyze, plan, monitor, and regulate their learning:

1. Teach the *what, how, when,* and *why* conditions of the strategies. For example, after teaching students about interview preparation (a data-gathering strategy), students should be able to answer at least the following questions: *What* can I do to be prepared? *What* should I not do? *How* can I make sure I am prepared? *How* can I use what my teacher taught me? *When*

should I use these strategies? *Why* are these the best ways? *Why* will the interview be more successful if I use these strategies?

2. Review and reteach the strategies, as necessary. Teachers can monitor and evaluate students to determine whether content or strategies need to be reviewed and retaught. Poor student outcomes result from confusion with either or both. For example, tables might be incomplete because students did not understand the topic well enough to select all the important information or because they skimmed the content in a careless and hurried manner. Teachers who observed these students while they gathered and recorded data will know whether the content or the strategies caused the problem and, therefore, what to review and reteach.

3. Convince students that their understanding and retention will increase when appropriate strategies are used consistently. Ideally, the first strategies taught should be those that will have an obvious effect on students' understanding, retention, grades, participation, or other outcomes valued by the teachers and students. Students benefit if the relationship between these outcomes and their strategy selection and use is discussed.

4. Use familiar and motivational content when introducing and teaching the strategies. Initial instruction using content students believe is difficult or irrelevant can cause negative first impressions to data and the research process. When teaching students how to understand a bar graph, for example, teachers should use data that relate to students personally to motivate them to listen to and then follow instructions. Students will truly want to learn what the data "say" if they are gathering and recording information about their favorite musical groups or how to spend $1,000. Their prior knowledge and past experiences with the topics will also help them understand and use the data. Once students are successful, they will be willing and able to use the same strategies to understand, make, and use bar graphs for course topics.

5. Provide abundant opportunities for students to use and practice the strategies. Students who gather, record, understand, and use data frequently internalize the strategies. This makes the tasks easier and more enjoyable. They are able to pay attention to what the data mean and concentrate less on mechanical procedures for manipulating the data.

6. Use the data strategies in purposeful and meaningful ways. Students' motivation and understanding will increase when they hear teachers talk about how and why they use particular strategies. For example, when teaching students not to skip charts in social studies textbooks, teachers might bring in a chart from a newspaper and explain why they took the time to study it, how they learned from it, and how they will use the information.

> *Students will truly want to learn what the data "say" if they are gathering and recording information about their favorite musical groups or how to spend $1,000.*

7. Ask questions about the data strategies students used to get their answers to determine whether review and reteaching of strategies or content are necessary and which strategies to teach next. Possible questions using the word 'learn' follow. Teachers can substitute such verbs as 'gather', 'record', 'understand', and 'use':

> How did you learn it?
> Why did you learn it that way?
> Did you like learning it that way? Why or why not?
> What strategies did you use?
> How did you know which strategies to use?
> Was it easy or hard to learn? Why?
> Will you use the same strategies next time? Why?

8. Give specific feedback about students' choices of strategies and the accuracy and the ease with which they use them. They deserve to know what and why they are doing well so they can repeat the same behavior. Students who struggle when working with data need to know specifically what they can change so they will choose more appropriate strategies and use them more efficiently and effectively. Sample feedback directed to strategy choice and use includes:

> Your answers are right. I think it helped that you_____.
> I think you did better recording these data because you_____.
> I think you made your mistake because_____. Next time, try_____.
> Your decision about where to look for data was smart because_____.
> You are forgetting how to do it right because you need to practice reading more pie graphs. I will help you practice with these. Remember to start here.
> You forgot to use the data collected yesterday. It would have helped you answer this question. Maybe you forgot to use it because you_____.

Conclusion

Readers are encouraged to pause now to think of one or more topics relevant to their social studies curricula, assignments, goals for students, and strategies from each phase of the social studies data process that students could use independently. Going through the chapter once again with these specific and personally relevant ideas in mind will help the readers set goals and try the most appropriate aspects of strategic thinking with their students.

References

Burns, P.C., B.D. Roe, and E.P. Ross. *Teaching Reading in Today's Elementary Schools*. Boston, Massachusetts: Houghton Mifflin, 1988.

Cook, D.M. *A Guide to Curriculum Planning in Reading*. Madison, Wisconsin: Wisconsin Department of Public Instruction, 1986.

Dechant, E.V. *Improving the Teaching of Reading*, 3d ed. Englewood Cliffs, New Jersey: Prentice-Hall, 1982.

Devine, T.G. *Teaching Study Skills: A Guide for Teachers*, 2d ed. Boston, Massachusetts: Allyn and Bacon, 1987.

Jones, B.F., A.S. Palincsar, D.S. Ogle, and E.G. Carr. *Strategic Teaching and Learning: Cognitive Instruction in the Content Areas*. Washington, D.C.: Association for Supervision and Curriculum Development, 1987.

Paris, S.G., M.Y. Lipson, and K.K. Wixson. "Becoming a Strategic Reader." *Contemporary Educational Psychology* 8 (1983): 293–316.

Summers, E.G. "Utilizing Visual Aids in Reading Materials for Effective Reading." In *Developing Study Skills in Secondary Schools*, ed. H.L. Herber. Newark, Delaware: International Reading Association, 1965: 97–156.

Strategic Thinking in the Social Studies

"Information-literate people have learned how to learn."

Information Age Quotation

"Information-literate people are those who have learned how to learn. They know how to learn because they know how knowledge is organized, how to find information, and how to use information in such a way that others learn from them. They are people prepared for lifelong learning, because they can always find the information needed for any task or decision at hand." —American Library Association, "Final Report of the ALA Presidential Committee on Information Literacy" (unpublished), 1989, 2.

"Now, knowledge—not minerals or agricultural products—is this country's most precious commodity, and people who are information-literate—who know how to acquire knowledge and use it—are America's most valuable resource." Ibid., 18.

"Citizenship in a modern democracy involves more than knowledge how to access vital information. It also involves a capacity to recognize propaganda, distortion, and other misuses of information." Ibid., 9.

Chapter 4

Civic Decision Making in an Information Age
Richard C. Remy

For as long as humans have lived in groups, they have had to make civic decisions—decisions about the governance of the groups in which they live. In the United States we have never been satisfied to leave such decisions, as Plato would have, to an enlightened elite. We have rather had faith in the power of schooling to educate citizens to think for themselves about issues, policies, and officials in government. From Thomas Jefferson to Horace Mann and John Dewey, we have believed that schools can prepare young people to participate in making civic decisions.

United States society and the world, however, have changed since Dewey's time. Rapid advances in science and technology, along with an explosion of information, pose new challenges for citizenship education. Many experts doubt the possibility of educating citizens to participate in deciding complex public policy issues of the Information Age. One nuclear physicist, for instance, says that "it is hopeless to try to educate the public on atomic energy, considering that the public is so uneducated in other subjects" (Browne 1979).

> *Public policy issues today involve vast quantities of technical information, great uncertainty, and many contending groups with conflicting values.*

The pervasive, powerful effects of the information explosion generated by science and technology pose a serious challenge to citizenship educators who wish to sustain the Jeffersonian ideal of self-government in modern society. What features of public policy issues in the modern era must we take into account for educating students to make informed decisions as citizens of local, state, national, and global communities? What model of civic decision making will accommodate such features and provide the basis for practical teaching strategies in the classroom?

Public Policy Decisions in the Modern Age

Why is it so difficult to deal with public policy issues in our information-rich age? When citizens or policymakers must choose between two or more courses of action, what makes it difficult to see clearly which choice is best? There are three features of modern public policy issues that turn many decisions into dilemmas.

Uncertain Consequences. Decision making about public policy issues nearly always involves uncertainty about the likely social, political, or environmental consequences of alternative courses of action. Decision theorists refer to such situations as decision making with risk (Schlaifer 1969; Hill 1979). By 'risk' they mean that one has incomplete knowledge of possible outcomes of a choice; though possibly enough knowledge to make some assessment of the probability of the consequences for a particular alternative.

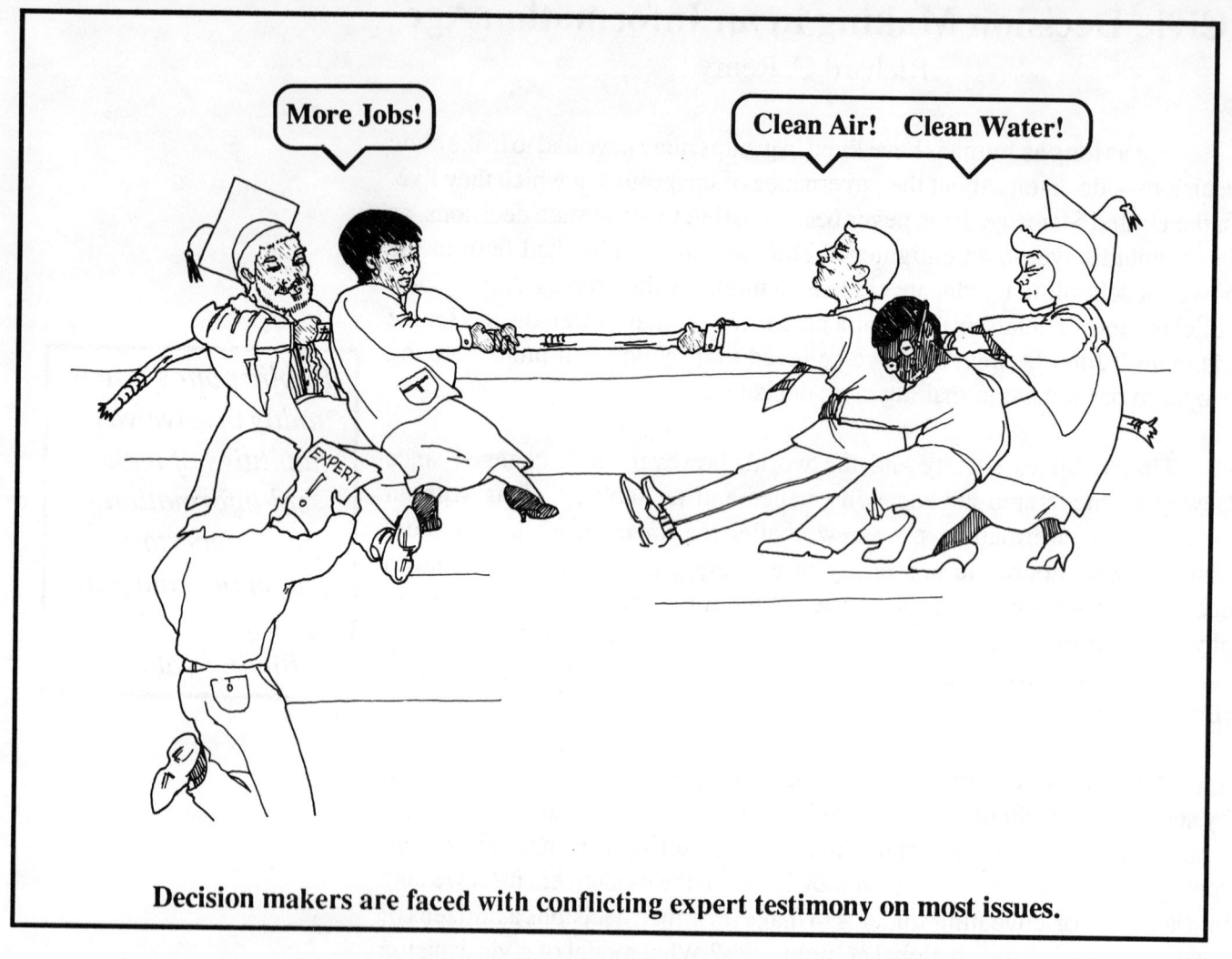

Civic Decision Making in an Information Age

Decision makers are faced with conflicting expert testimony on most issues.

The number of such decisions has increased exponentially as the public policy agenda have become filled with complex issues generated by advances in science and technology (Miller et al. 1985). Experimentation with DNA, *in vitro* fertilization, control of nuclear weapons, disposal of toxic wastes, euthanasia, limits on industrial development, and genetic screening for employment are only a few of the types of issues generated by science and technology. New policy issues will continue to emerge at an ever-increasing pace.

Without certain or nearly certain knowledge, disagreements may, and usually do, arise over the precise consequences of alternative public policies toward such issues. The debate, for example, over Senate approval of the Intermediate-Range Nuclear Forces (INF) Treaty between the Soviet Union and the United States revolved in large part over whether the treaty would ultimately ensure Europe's security. No one could say for sure.

Conflicting Expert Testimony. All this is not to say that citizens today lack information about various positions on public policy issues. Indeed, the hallmark of the Information Age is that we are inundated by factual claims and data that support conflicting positions in public policy issues and the possible consequences of their various alternatives. The problem is that our increased ability to generate and disseminate information has combined with the uncertainty arising from the technological complexity of many public policy issues to create a situation where decision makers are faced with conflicting expert testimony on most issues.

Contending groups often marshal technical and scientific expertise to support their position on an issue. Environmentalists hire experts to present data about the likelihood of thermal pollution from a new power plant. Power plant supporters have their own experts testify on the technical feasibility of a project. After listening to more than 120 scientists argue about the safety of nuclear power, the California state legislature, for example, decided that the issues were not, after all, resolvable by expertise alone (Nelkin 1979). Conflicting expert opinion and huge amounts of information available on most issues pose a real dilemma for citizens and policymakers alike.

Complex Value Trade-offs. Public policy decisions today often require 'trade-offs' between conflicting values in which no clear view of right or wrong can readily be derived from the facts no matter how many data on the issue are available. In disputes about abortion, the so-called creation science, or various nuclear power plant disputes, no amount of factual data is likely to settle the basic value conflicts involved.

> *We can ... help students take into account the uncertainties, complexity, factual claims, and value conflicts involved in decision making.*

Many environmental issues today, for example, require citizens and policymakers to choose between clean water and air or production and jobs. Nearly everyone agrees that pollution by factories is bad. People also agree that unemployment and large declines in industrial productivity are bad. The problem has been to decide how to limit pollution to protect health and environment while still maintaining production and jobs. Decision making about such issues requires careful consideration of alternative factual and value claims. The choice in such a situation may eventually result from a compromise between conflicting positions about values.

Even when decisions are made under conditions of reasonable certainty, people may opt for particular solutions because they value the outcomes differently (Bursts et al. 1981). Some people will choose to smoke tobacco and others will not do so in the face of known health risks. Some groups argue for continued federal subsidies for tobacco farmers while others call for an end to the subsidies. In the latter case, few people seriously dispute the growing scientific evidence on the health dangers of smoking. However, people evaluate public health and promoting a segment of the economy differently.

A Decision-Making Model for the Information Age

We can derive from social science a model of decision making that can help students take into account the uncertainties, complexities, factual claims, and value conflicts involved in civic decision making today. The model specifies the basic cognitive operations involved in making such choices. It thus provides a useful conceptual map for developing programs that will ensure student competence with making decisions in an Information Age.

Four cognitive operations involved in any civic or social decision are (1) understanding the need for choice—the occasion for making a decision, (2) identifying the values and goals involved in the decision, (3) identifying alternative responses to the occasion for decision, and (4) predicting positive or negative consequences of alternatives in terms of values and goals involved in the decision (Remy et al. 1989; Fulcher 1965).

> *The decision tree ... involves interlacing knowledge drawn from social studies with the arts of critical thinking and judgment.*

An occasion for making a decision is a problem situation in which a solution is not obvious and choice may be required, including the possibility of doing nothing in response to the problem. Identifying values and goals involves asking, What is important to me? What do I want, and what is right or wrong in this situation? Decision makers express value judgments when labeling consequences such as loss of jobs from closing a polluting factory as good or bad. When setting goals, decision makers engage in clarification of values. Identifying alternative courses of action involves thinking about the facts; it means asking, What are possible solutions? What can be done? Predicting likely consequences of alternatives involves gathering information and sorting out competing factual claims about likely outcomes.

These four operations may be used unequally in different situations. We may sometimes be able to identify alternatives easily but it may be difficult to rank-order our values and goals. At times, the core of the decision-making task may be to think creatively of alternatives to reach a clear and long-standing goal. At still other times, we may clearly know what alternatives are available and what goal we want to reach, but the challenge is to predict accurately the consequences of alternatives.

Practical Classroom Applications

As we have seen, public policy issues today involve vast quantities of technical information, great uncertainty, and contending groups with conflicting values. We have identified key elements in making decisions about such issues. How can we make these elements tangible so that students can learn systematically about and develop competence in decision making?

One useful strategy is a procedure called the decision tree. This device was originally created by Roger LaRaus and Richard Remy as an adaptation for precollege students of the more complex problem-solving routine of the same name that is widely used in social science decision theory, engineering, management science, and—increasingly—in medical science and education (LaRaus and Remy 1978; Hill 1979; Raiffa 1970; Behn and Vaupel 1982). Since its creation, the decision tree has been successfully applied in several major curriculum projects (Patrick and Remy 1984, 1986; Remy et al. 1989).

For precollege students, the procedure can be represented by a chart in the form of a tree with several branches that suggest the connections between various alternatives, consequences, and values of the decision maker. By using a chart depicting a decision tree, students can practice skills in clarifying and making choices about a wide range of public issues and policies. As shown in Figure 1, the decision tree includes the essential elements of decision making discussed previously. These elements involve interlacing knowledge drawn from social studies with the arts of critical thinking and judgment.

The decision tree in Figure 1 is part of a textbook in junior high school civics (Patrick and Remy 1986). Figure 1 shows moves students make to analyze a real land-use decision faced by the Navajo in Black Mesa, Arizona. Students start at the trunk of the tree or "occasion for decision"—in this instance, the discovery of large deposits of shallow vein, low-sulfur coal on the Navajo reservation. They next identify the alternatives considered by the Navajo and then move into the branches to map possible negative or positive consequences of each alternative. When considering these consequences, they make factual judgments about the likely outcomes of each alternative. They also consider what is good or bad about these consequences in terms of values and goals they have assigned to the problem at the top of the tree. This consideration of good and bad requires critical thinking, ethical reasoning, and value judgments by the students.

Social studies educators can use decision trees with elementary through senior high school students to help students

- study current or historical decisions by government officials on issues at local, state, national, and international level
- analyze complex social, political, economic, and technological issues
- practice and apply critical information acquisition and thinking skills in a real context
- practice making their own decisions regarding real or simulated public policy issues

Civic Decision Making in an Information Age

Figure 1. The Decision Tree

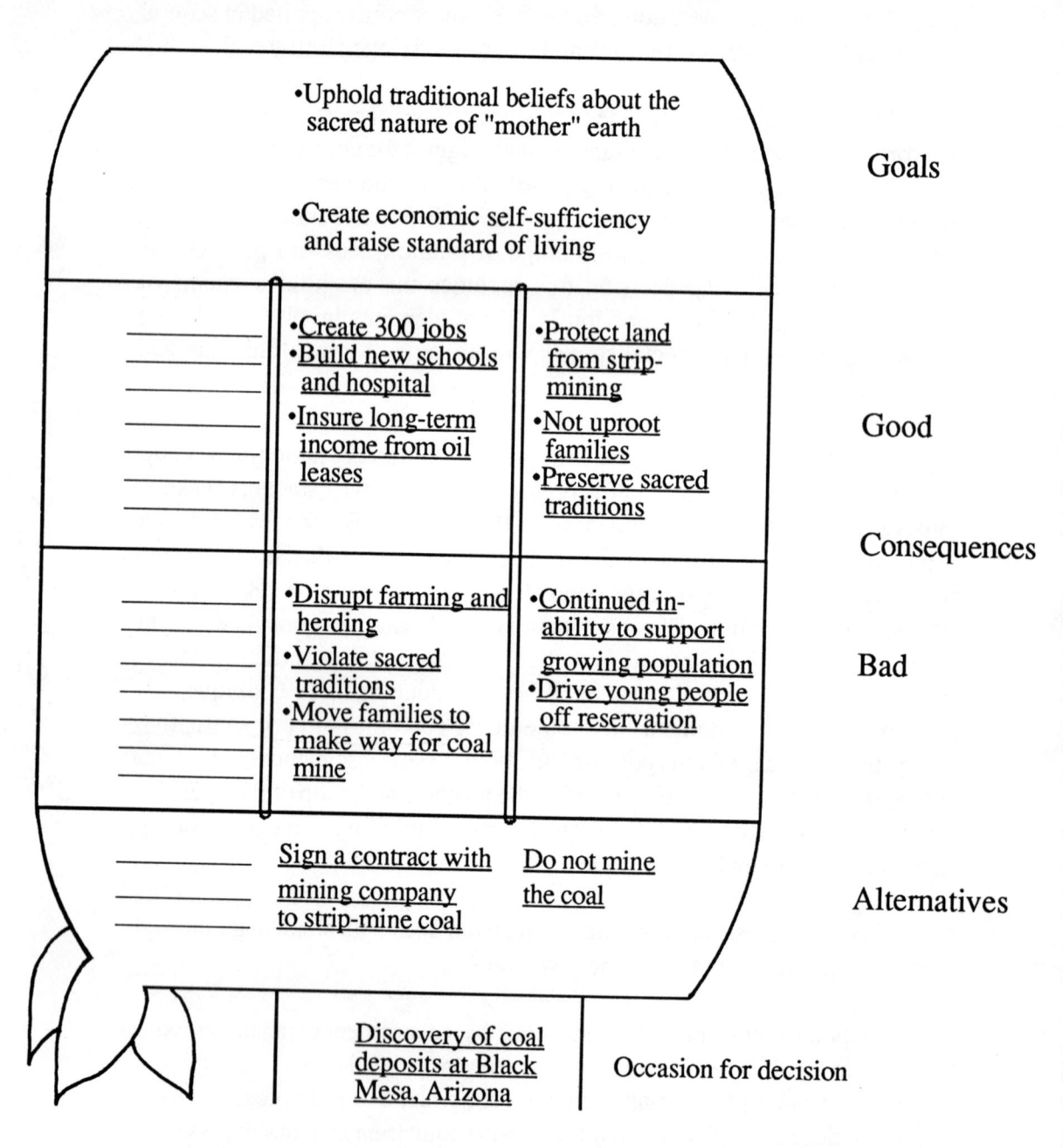

Goals
- Uphold traditional beliefs about the sacred nature of "mother" earth
- Create economic self-sufficiency and raise standard of living

Good Consequences
- Create 300 jobs
- Build new schools and hospital
- Insure long-term income from oil leases
- Protect land from strip-mining
- Not uproot families
- Preserve sacred traditions

Bad Consequences
- Disrupt farming and herding
- Violate sacred traditions
- Move families to make way for coal mine
- Continued inability to support growing population
- Drive young people off reservation

Alternatives
- Sign a contract with mining company to strip-mine coal
- Do not mine the coal

Occasion for decision
- Discovery of coal deposits at Black Mesa, Arizona

The decision tree device used on this page was developed by Roger La Raus and Richard C. Remy. The device is used in this text with their permission.

Models like that of the decision tree may be used to pattern instruction on decision making into the curriculum from intermediate grades through senior high school, providing iteration without boring repetition. Students continually repeat skills and critical-thinking processes while wrestling with increasingly sophisticated decision problems from the politics and governance of their everyday life and from the adult political world. This type of iteration without boring repetition provides practice in decision-making skills and opportunity for students to learn at their own rate.

References

Behn, R.D., and R.D. Vaupel. *Quick Analysis for Busy Decision Makers*. New York: Basic Books, 1982.

Browne, M. "The Untutored Public." *New York Times*, April 22, 1979, 14.

Bursts, H., et al. *Medical Choices, Medical Chances: How Patients, Families, and Physicians Can Cope with Uncertainty*. New York: Delacorte Press/Seymour Lawrence, 1981.

Fulcher, Gordon S. *Common Sense Decision Making*. Evanston, Illinois: Northwestern University Press, 1965.

Hill, P.H., ed. *Making Decisions: A Multidisciplinary Approach*. Reading, Massachusetts: Addison-Wesley, 1979.

LaRaus, R., and R.C. Remy. *Citizenship Decision Making: Skill Activities and Materials*. Reading, Massachusetts: Addison-Wesley, 1978.

Miller, J.D., R.W. Suchner, and A. Voelker. *Citizenship in an Age of Science*. Elmsford, New York: Pergamon Press, 1985.

Nelkin, D., ed. *Controversy: Politics of Technical Decisions*. Beverly Hills, California: Sage Publications, 1979.

Patrick, J.J., and R.C. Remy. *Lessons on the Constitution*. Washington, D.C.: Project '87, American Historical Association, American Political Science Association, 1984.

Patrick, J.J., and R.C. Remy. *Civics for Americans*. Glenview, Illinois: Scott, Foresman, 1986.

Raiffa, H. *Decision Analysis: Introductory Lectures on Choices under Uncertainty*. Reading, Massachusetts: Addison-Wesley, 1970.

Remy, R.C., J.E. Harf, and B.T. Trout. *Teaching about National Security: Instructional Strategies and Lessons for Courses in History, Government, Geography, and Economics.* Reading, Massachusetts: Addison-Wesley, 1989.

Remy, R. C. "Making, Judging, and Influencing Political Decisions: A Focus for Citizenship Education." *Social Education* 40 (October 1976): 360–65.

Schlaifer, R. *Analysis of Decisions under Uncertainty.* New York: McGraw-Hill, 1969.

Information Age Quotations

"The new world of the future is already upon us. The changes brought by information technology cannot be put into a single headline, but they are all around us.

• High in the Andes, a homemade satellite dish in an Indian village pulls in television programs from Argentina.

• In Guatemala City, televiewers watch the Atlanta-based Cable News Network (CNN). And I might say when I went to Beijing earlier this year, I turned on the TV, and there was CNN. Talk about an information standard.

• In central Brazil, soybean growers receive real-time data on Chicago Board trading by computer.

• In Barbados and Dominican Republic, key-entry operators encode information from tons of library catalogs and court transcripts, telephone directories and manufacturing inventories flown in daily by jet from all over the world. In a matter of hours, the same data is on its way—this time electronically—to data banks abroad." —George C. Shultz, *Department of State Bulletin,* December 1988, 13.

"The information revolution is changing our global economy, transforming national political and business institutions, and altering national foreign policy objectives and the methods of achieving them. Just as the spread of rudimentary medical knowledge took away the power of the witch doctor, the spread of information about alternative life-styles in other countries threatens the validity of some official doctrines and thus some government's power bases.

"Knowledge has always conferred power on those who have it and know how to use it, and the proliferation and dissemination of information to huge numbers of people can be, and more often is, a precursor to a shift in the power structure. But the effects of the information revolution go even deeper: the very nature and definition of national sovereignty is being altered." —Walter W. Wriston, "Technology and Sovereignty," *Foreign Affairs* (Fall 1988): 65.

Chapter 5

Using Census Data in Elementary and Secondary Social Studies Programs: A Timely Example

George Dailey and
Leah Engelhardt

April 1, 1990, will mark a special anniversary—the bicentennial of the census of population in the United States. The nation's census had its birth in Article 1, Section 2, of the Constitution. In keeping with the constitutional mandate, the first census was conducted in 1790 and repeated every 10 years thereafter. The 1990 census will complete a 200-year, unbroken span of periodic enumerations of population in the United States. Since 1940, the decennial census also has included the Census of Housing. Together they will make the 1990 census the single largest data-collection and statistical operation in the nation's history.

Fact finder for the nation!

This chapter focuses on the 1990 census and a new interdisciplinary K–12 teaching package developed as part of the celebration—the 1990 Census Education Project. This chapter also provides background on the U.S. Bureau of the Census and a taste of the variety of information and resource material available from this agency and gives ideas of how census data and concepts can enrich social studies teaching.

Start with these recent demographic headlines:

Census Bureau Estimates Average Congressional District Population Was 553,000 in 1986 (January 25, 1988)	Farm Population Continues to Shrink in the 1980s (July 20, 1988)
Voting Age Population Will Total 183 Million This November (February 3, 1988)	Preprimary School Enrollment Up but Elementary and Secondary Down since 1981 (September 8, 1988)
Three States Likely to Provide Half of U.S. Population Growth into the Next Century (April 1, 1988)	About Half the U.S. Population Lives in Metro(politan) Areas of a Million or More (September 30, 1988)
Two-Worker Families with Children Increasing (June 16, 1988)	Births, Immigrants Boost U.S. Population above 245 Million (October 5, 1988)

Numeric trivia? Necessary ammunition for armchair contestants of "Jeopardy"? For some, yes. These press-release headlines and associated stories, however, speak more importantly of the nation's political, socioeconomic, geographic, and educational present and of implications for the future. These data are from one source—the U.S. Bureau of the Census.

Fact Finder for the Nation

> ### Census Bureau Mission
> *In its best interests, a civilized nation counts and profiles its people and institutions. Doing so ably and objectively is the abiding mission of the United States Census Bureau. We honor privacy, shun partisanship, invite scrutiny, and share our expertise globally. Striving to excel, we chronicle the Nation's past, describe its present, and illuminate its future.*

The Bureau of the Census, created in 1902, is known as the "Fact Finder for the Nation." The name is very appropriate because the agency constantly collects data and provides information. The Census Bureau is best known for the national census of population and housing every 10 years (in years ending in 0), but it also conducts national economic, agriculture, and government censuses every five years (in years ending in 2 and 7). Besides censuses, the agency administers about 250 sample surveys each year, many for other federal agencies, and prepares estimates and projections.

This collection of facts yields a wide variety of products. Statistics are available in printed reports (with tables, charts, and maps), on microfiche, computer diskettes and tapes, wall maps, and through a new on-line data service—CENDATA. The data are provided for a wide range of geographic units (e.g., the nation, states, American Indian reservations, and Alaska Native villages, cities, counties, neighborhoods, and blocks). Some publications, such as the *Statistical Abstract of the United States* and the *County and City Data Book*, also combine facts from many sources into handy statistical references.

Real-World Information

Census facts and figures are an important part of everyday living. They tell us who we are, how and where we live, how we are housed, what changes are taking place in the socioeconomic fabric of the country, and to a large degree what the future will be like. Besides describing a nation, its people, and institutions, these numbers guide inquiry and decisions of personal, local, and national significance on a daily basis. The headline that three states (California, Texas, and Florida) are projected to lead the way in total U.S. population growth into the 21st century has far-reaching implications; for instance, this growth will help shape the future makeup of the House of Representatives.

The implications and applications of census information affect everyone. The number of applications and the variety of agencies and persons using the data are increasing. Given the increasing size of the population and the complexity of American society, more decision makers are finding that major plans, especially those involving monetary investments, are facilitated by using census data.

Governments draw heavily on census data in planning and implementing community projects, such as planning for new schools. The 1990 census population totals will be used for reapportionment and to determine congressional, state, and local election district boundaries. Business and industry use these statistics, especially those for small geographic areas, in deciding plant and office locations, expansions, and the like. An increasing number of social service providers have found that census facts give the kind of assistance they need in reaching and helping their clientele. Through the 1980 Census Neighborhood Statistics Program, census information was made available for approximately 28,000 neighborhoods, giving community leaders an improved understanding of the needs of their areas. Finally, more individuals are using census information to guide decisions of personal importance such as planning a small business or helping choose a new area of a community in which to live.

Census Data, Census Concepts, and Classroom Objectives

These same data and concepts used by a variety of community institutions can also become a key part of the social studies classroom and help teachers meet curriculum objectives. Besides helping to strengthen student thinking and analysis skills, making use of census information in the classroom adds another dimension to specific objectives and fundamental themes including

- learning time terms, such as decade
- learning a part of civic responsibility, since participation in the decennial census is a requirement in our democracy
- understanding the effect of the size, composition, and distribution of the population on historic events and institutions and vice versa
- understanding changes in the economic system
- becoming better equipped to understand the fundamental geographic themes of location, place, relationships within places, movement, and regions
- understanding the basic organization of the federal government and the U.S. political system
- understanding and using such sociological concepts as family, neighborhood, community, race and ethnicity, and ascribed and achieved population characteristics as gender and educational attainment, for example

The implications and applications of census information affect everyone.

Exposing students to census taking and census data and concepts will not only help them become more effective citizens but will also broaden their career possibilities in market research, statistics, policy analysis, social sciences, and computer programming.

Using Census Data in Social Studies: A Timely Example

The Decennial Census as a Classroom Focus

The upcoming 1990 census provides an excellent opportunity to introduce or reinforce the three themes of this bulletin—data gathering, data interpretation, and civic decision making. At the same time, the 1990 census, both as a national-local current event and as a part of the ongoing history of the nation, provides a framework around which to introduce the activities of and the wealth of information produced by the Bureau of the Census.

An Historical Perspective. Census taking is a very old practice. Throughout history, nations have used censuses of their populations to measure occupations and potential military strength and for taxation purposes. On the North American continent, enumeration has a long heritage. It has been an accounting tool for Indian peoples inhabiting the continent and for subsequent European colonial immigrants in such areas as New Spain, New France, and the English colonies. In the English colonies alone, about 40 censuses were taken.

From its beginning, the U.S. Census has been more than a simple head count.

The need for a national census of the new United States arose soon after the 13 colonies broke their ties with Great Britain. The costs of the Revolutionary War had been high. The new nation had to find ways to pay the debt; one way was to divide it equally among the people. (Note: Although constitutionally planned, counting for taxation never did occur.) Another reason for a census was to establish a truly representative government to sit in the two houses of Congress. Although each state, regardless of size, would have two senators in the Senate, the number of members of the House of Representatives would be apportioned among the states according to their population. The only way to find out how many people there were was to count them; so for the first time in history, a nation decided to make a census part of its constitution. As adopted in 1787, the United States Constitution included these words in Article 1, Section 2:

> The actual Enumeration shall be made within three Years after the first Meeting of the Congress of the United States and within every subsequent Term of ten Years, in such Manner as they shall by Law direct.

With these words, the decennial census of the United States was born.

The first census recorded very limited information. Under the Census Act of 1790, the count was to ascertain the number of inhabitants in various geographic groupings, omitting American Indians not taxed, and distinguishing free persons (including those bound to service for a term of years) from all others; the sex and color of free persons; and the number of free males 16 years of age and over.

From its beginning, the decennial census has been more than a simple head count. Gathering information on sex and age in 1790 was done to obtain knowledge of the military and industrial strength of the country. Throughout the years, the nation has changed and so has the decennial census. The size, composition, and distribution of the population; the laws; and the complexity of the country have changed, and with them, the need for statistical information. To stay in step, the content of the census has varied over time. Since 1940, the decennial census has been limited to items on population and housing. (See Figure 1 for a sample of data reported in censuses from 1790 to 1980. The chart is an excerpt from Handout 3 of Activity 10 in the *1990 Census Education Project* teaching kit. Figure 2 from Activity 6 gives a picture of the movement and expansion of our population in each census.)

Collecting 1990 Census Information. The task of taking the census in 1990 will be more complex than it was in 1790 and at any time since. Just under 4 million persons and little more than a half million households were counted in the 1790 census. Since that time, the country has grown dramatically, but the time allowed to complete a census and report its findings is very limited. The Census Bureau anticipates that the

Figure 1.
Historical Census Data of the United States

Year	Population (in thousands)	Places of 50,000 or More Persons	Median Age	Males per 100 Females	Non-Agricultural Workers per 100 Agricultural Workers [1]	High School Graduates Percent of Persons Age 17 or Over	High School Graduates Percent of Persons Age 25 or Over	Average Number of Persons per Household
1790	3,929	0		104[2]				5.79
1800	5,308	1	16.0[2]	104[2]				
1810	7,240	2	16.0[2]	104[2]				
1820	9,638	3	16.7	103				
1830	12,866	4	17.2	103				
1840	17,069	5	17.8	104	29			
1850	23,192	10	18.9	104				5.55
1860	31,443	16	19.4	105				5.28
1870	39,818	25	20.2	102	94	2.0		5.09
1880	50,156	35	20.9	104	125	2.5		5.04
1890	62,948	58	22.0	105	155	3.5		4.93
1900	75,995	78	22.9	104	180	6.3		4.76
1910	91,972	110	24.1	106	208	8.6		4.54
1920	105,711	145	25.3	104	290	16.3		4.34
1930	122,775	192	26.4	103	366	28.8		4.11
1940	131,669	200	29.0	101	433	49.0	24.5	3.67
1950	150,697	233[3]	30.2	99	711	57.4	34.3	3.37
1960[4]	179,323	333[3]	29.5	97	1,418	63.4	41.1	3.33
1970	203,302	396[3]	28.0	95	2,684	75.6	52.3	3.14
1980	226,546	463[3]	30.0	95	3,437		66.5	2.75

[1] 1840 data included all persons, all ages; 1870-1930, persons age 10 and over; 1940-1960, persons age 14 and over; and 1970-1980, persons age 16 and over.
[2] White only.
[3] Using current urban definition.
[4] Denotes first year for which figures here include Alaska and Hawaii.
Sources: Bureau of the Census. *Historical Statistics of the United States, Colonial Times to 1970; 1987 Statistical Abstract; 1980 Census of Population, Vol. 1, Chapter A 1960, 1970, 1980 Census of Housing, Vol. 1, Chapter A; 1840 Census of Population.*

Using Census Data in Social Studies: A Timely Example

Center of Population

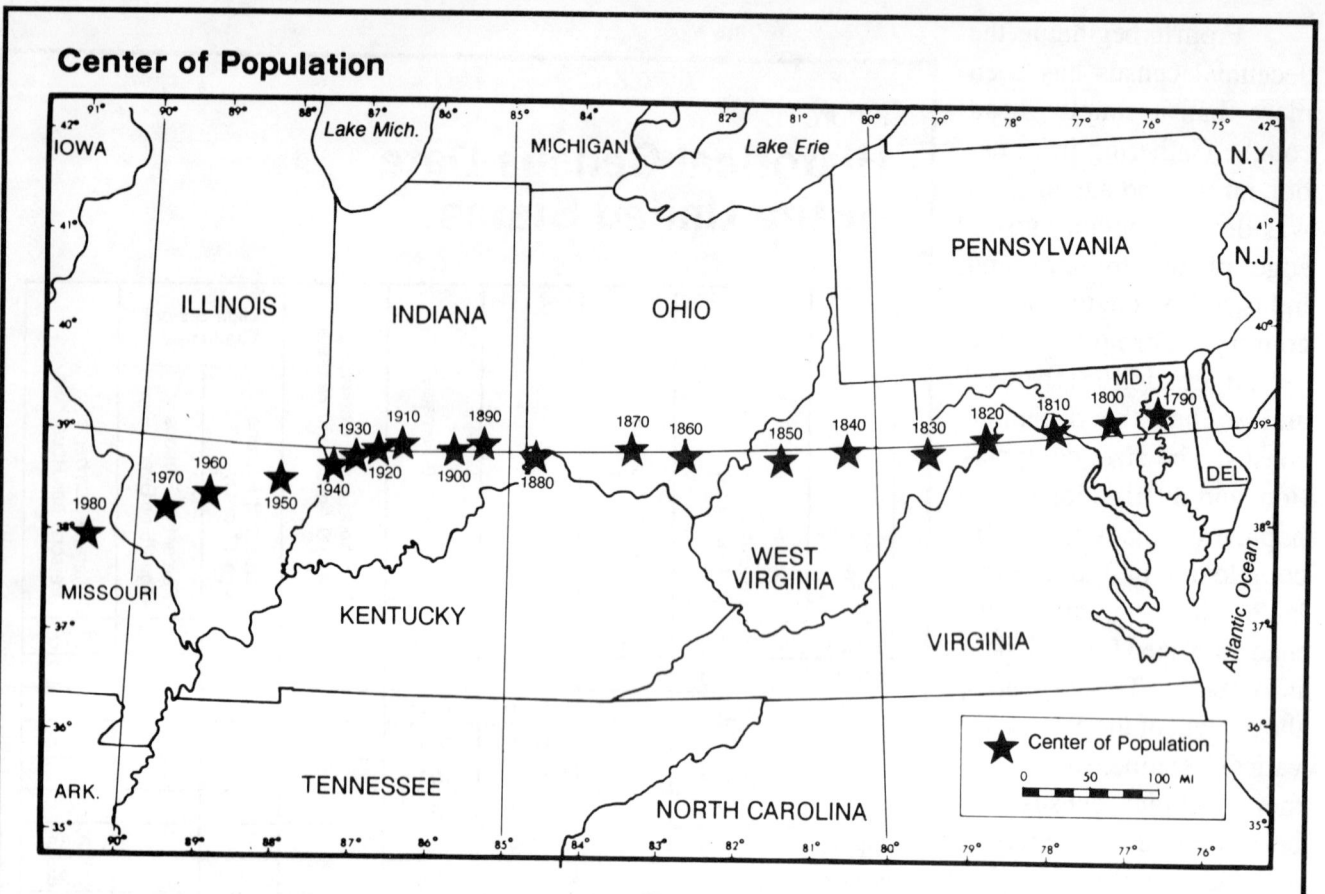

The "Center of Population" is that point at which the country would balance perfectly if it were a flat surface and every person on it had an equal weight.

U.S. population will approach 250 million people by 1990. It is also expected that the number of housing units will be about 106 million. The agency must collect the required information about all these people and their housing as of April 1, 1990, follow up where there is need, edit the questionnaires, partially process the forms, summarize a portion of the data, and report state and United States population totals to the president by December 31, 1990—or within nine months. After completing this mandate, processing will be completed and the full complement of 1990 data and products will be generated during the years of the following decade.

Most households in the nation will receive a census questionnaire in the mail shortly before Census Day—April 1, 1990. Census enumerators will personally deliver the questionnaire in some rural areas and in some large urban multifamily apartment complexes. All census forms (questionnaires) are to be completed to represent each household's composition and characteristics as of Census Day. Completed forms should include everyone who *usually* lives in the household but exclude persons only visiting. Babies born before midnight of Census Day are included.

Nearly 95 percent of the nation's households will be asked to return the completed form in the mail right away. The remainder, residing in sparsely settled rural areas and in special places and group quarters (such as nursing homes, college dormitories, military barracks, and boarding houses), will have a census taker visit to pick up the completed forms or to complete a form in an interview. If a household was supposed to return the form by mail but did not, a census enumerator, one of 400,000 temporary workers to be hired, must then go to that home and obtain the information.

Nationwide, most households will receive a short census form asking only a limited number of questions about each household member (such as race, Spanish origin, age, and marital status) and characteristics about the housing unit (such as owner or renter status). On the average, this form will take about 15–20 minutes to complete.

The remaining households will receive a form that will contain more questions about the members of the household (for example, education, employment, income, occupation, and ancestry) and the housing unit (for example, age of the building, source of water, type of fuel used for heating). The average completion time for this form will be about 45 minutes. These households will be selected by a sampling pattern. Responses from these sample households will be very important, because these answers will statistically depict the total population on such items as education. This sampling method will be used to minimize demands made on the public, while producing useful and reliable data.

Answering the Census: Civic Duty, Confidentiality, and the Law. Since this census happens only once every ten years, it is an event easily forgotten and frequently misunderstood by many. The purpose of the census is to obtain counts—statistical totals. Questions are asked of individuals and households to compile these totals. Only questions which address important policy and program needs are included "in such Manner as they shall by Law direct." Answering census questions is a civic responsibility. It is also the law (as mandated in Title 13 of the United States Code since 1954). Failure to comply can result in penalties, including fines of up to $500. This same law keeps answers given in the census away from welfare agencies, the Immigration and Naturalization Service, the Internal Revenue Service, courts, police, the military, and everyone else. The 1990 census records will be held confidential for 72 years—until the year 2062. Only the records from 1790 to 1910 are now open to the public.

No one—neither a census taker nor any other employee of the Census Bureau—can reveal information about any individual or family to anyone outside the Census Bureau. Census workers swear an oath to uphold this confidence. Census employees violating the oath are subject to severe penalties of up to five years in prison or $5,000 in fines.

Using Census Data in Social Studies: A Timely Example

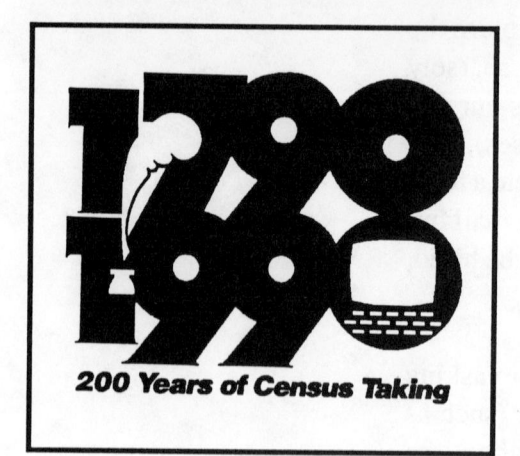

The integrity of census confidentiality also has been upheld in court. Legal challenges from outside the Census Bureau for access to actual census forms and other protected material (such as address lists) have all been denied. This tough stand on confidentiality is a hallmark of census taking in the United States.

After the 1980 census, the Census Bureau estimated that a small percentage of the population had not been counted. This undercount was higher among minority populations. Some people were missed because they left themselves out of the census. Some were afraid, some did not care, and some did not realize that they were required to respond.

An undercount of segments of the population can have an adverse effect on decisions. Inaccuracies in the data can alter or halt projects and cause misallocations in the distribution of local funds and services. Some of these are designed for the very people who failed to be counted. Being missed in the census has an effect on the people missed as well as their neighbors who may be denied certain benefits. That is why it is important that people be made aware of the census and complete the census form.

1990 Census Education Project

The 1990 Census Education Project is one part of the Census Bureau's national outreach program for the 1990 census. The project is directed to all elementary and secondary schools and districts. The primary component of the project is a package of K–12 teacher-ready classroom activities, suggested lesson extensions, recommended community participation events and activities, and an annotated list of other census resources. The teaching materials are interdisciplinary in nature—bridging social studies, mathematics, science, and language arts. They also suggest ways of integrating classroom learning with parental and community involvement. A copy of the kit was mailed to schools nationwide in March 1989.

The objectives of the project are to provide teachers with innovative, reusable materials in their classroom teaching and to introduce educators and students to an important national event in which everyone needs to participate. The materials will help extend students' citizenship, history, geography, multicultural, critical thinking, computational, and statistical skills through a hands-on exposure to information and activities with real-world relevance. They will create an awareness and understanding of the importance of the census, the confidential nature of the individual answers, the uses of summarized census statistics, and, in general, how census data are a real part of everyone's life now and in the future.

Classroom Materials and Ideas. Space constraints, here, unfortunately preclude including of a complete teacher-ready activity from the 1990 kit. However, figures 2 through 4 provide an overview of the contents of the package, a few ideas from the "Extension/Enrichment Activities" sections in some of the lessons, and a sampler of other materials listed in the Teaching Resources Guide contained in each 1990 kit. Ordering information for a free copy of the *1990 Census Education Project* teaching kit can be found at the end of Figure 4.

Figure 2.
Overview of the 1990 Census Education Project
Teaching Kit Contents

Teacher-Ready Activities	Suggested Grades	Description
1 Taking a Census	K-2	Students learn what the census is and roleplay the census process. (Worksheet also in Spanish.)
2 Add! Don't Subtract!	2-6	Students learn the concepts of complete count and undercount, prepare a map, summarize data, and make decisions.
3 What Do You Know About the Census?	4-7	Key vocabulary terms and the history of the census in this country are introduced in a short reading. A quiz about the census and important census data is included. (Quiz and reading also in Spanish.)
4 Where Have We Been? Where Are We Going?	3-10	Students participate in a home and hobby survey (which may be customized by the class). They conduct the same survey, asking parents or other adults how things were in the past, and compare the results. (Survey also in Spanish.)
5 Would You Sell Snowshoes in Honolulu?	4-8	Students gain hands-on experience using census-like data as a basis for decisions about community services and businesses.
6 Lights! Camera! Action!	5-12	Students examine how U.S. population size and distribution have changed over twenty censuses. Population density, center of population, and historical causes for population change are considered.
7 State the States	6-12	Using a chart of recent census information (area and population) for all 50 states and the District of Columbia, students identify extreme cases and study changes over time.
8 That's Easy for You to Say!	7-12	Students study the process of designing, conducting, and analyzing the results of a survey and have the option to carry out a survey project.
9 Studying 1980 Census Snapshots	7-12	Students study a chart of selected 1980 census data for four cities and four counties, and discuss issues related to population density, business and community planning, and the housing industry. Local census data can be added.
10 200 Years and Counting	7-12	Students examine census data from twenty censuses and primary source documents to gain insight into changing data needs and a sense of the historical nature of the census in this country.
Educator's Guide to the 1990 Census		Guide provides background information about the census useful in answering student questions. It contains a glossary of census terms and basic placement and time of use information.
Teaching Resources Guide		Publication gives an annotated listing of selected Census Bureau products and information useful in the classroom including wall maps, special reports, statistical compendia, computer resources, ways of staying up-to-date, and a listing of where to find data and assistance in every state.
Suggested School and District Outreach Activities		Leaflet provides ideas of projects and events that classes, schools, and districts can undertake to generate community awareness about the upcoming census such as poster contests, historical exhibits, and media campaigns.

Figure 3.
Selected Classroom Activities
Excerpts From the 1990 Census Education Project
Teaching Kit, Extension/Enrichment Activities

From Activity 1
Have students do a count of the members of the class. Have them count and total the number of boys and girls, their ages, the types of housing they live in, or other characteristics. This could be done by having the students stand and form groups for the characteristic in question (girls on one side, boys on the other). Then have them regroup for the next characteristic and so forth. The totals for each item could be listed on the chalkboard. Then discuss the profile. Other items which you could investigate in this manner are the types of pets students have, their favorite TV shows, favorite colors, and so forth.

Develop a human graph by writing the words GIRLS and BOYS in two places on the chalkboard. Have the girls form a straight line in front of the word GIRLS and the boys in front of BOYS. Make a mark with chalk or tape in front of the first person in each line. Draw a bar graph of the information on the chalkboard to demonstrate how real people are depicted in symbolic form. Develop human graphs of other student characteristics.

From Activities 3 and 10
Have the students research the history surrounding the inclusion of the census in the Constitution and the Great Compromise of July 1787. Have students locate and read Article 1, Section 2 of the U.S. Constitution for the legal precedent on the census. Also have them read the 13th, 14th, and 16th amendments for constitutional changes affecting the census.

From Activity 4
To gain a visual understanding of how data change over time, have the students create a bulletin board display depicting their community today and in the past. Ask them to collect photographs and drawings of people, buildings, events that show change. Supplement this with population information from past censuses for the community. When assembled, have them write an essay about interesting facts displayed about their community.

From Activity 7
One of the major factors influencing state population change is migration—people moving into and out of a state. To help students better understand the mobile nature of the population, take a count of the moves (changes of residence) that students have made **across** state boundaries. List the different states on the chalkboard and tally the number of students who have lived in each. Have them create a percentage distribution of the information and map it. Ask them to consider the reasons why people move (such as to be closer to family, change jobs, retire, move to a bigger house, live in a different climate). Ask them why they moved.

Assign the study of U.S. migration as a small group research topic. Have the students examine major migration inducing events/phenomena in the Nation's history. Have them look at the social, economic, demographic, political, and/or environmental changes generated by the migration. Some topics to include are: Industrialization, the Decline of Farming, Black Migration to the North, the Trans Alaska Pipeline, the Dust Bowl, the formation of the Indian Territory, the California Goldrush.

From Activity 9
Have the students make extensive use of the 1983 or 1988 **County and City Data Book**. (See Figure 4 for details on this reference document.) Have them create data profiles and reports of various locations and/or do comparisons between locations. Ask them to develop profiles of each of the National Football League team locations and have them do comparisons throughout the season as teams play one another. As geographically tied events happen around the country, have the students create special profiles to better understand the event or the people it involves.

From Activity 10
Have them develop historical data profiles and graphic presentations of data for their community/state using census data and other resources. Have them create an historical exhibit as part of their 1990 census celebration. Have the students create a local history and publish it in the school newspaper. Invite a representative from your local historical society or similar group to assist. Ask the students if anyone in their family has produced a family history or genealogy. Invite those family members into the class to share their experiences. Have students research family members in the 1790-1910 census records.

Using Census Data in Social Studies: A Timely Example

Figure 4.
Sampler of Census Resources Available
Excerpt From Census Bureau Teaching Resources Guide

Factfinder for the Nation. *Factfinders* give topical overviews and explanations of Census Bureau products, programs, and concepts. A partial list follows.

Factfinder 2-	Availability of Census Records about Individuals
Factfinder 4-	History & Organization [of the Census & Census Bureau]
Factfinder 5-	Reference Sources
Factfinder 8-	Census Geography- Concepts & Products
Factfinder 18-	Census Bureau Programs & Products
Factfinder 22-	Data for Small Communities

Counting for Representation: The Census & The Constitution. This 8-page booklet examines the constitutional origin of the census, apportionment, the Census Bureau's role in this process, and changes that have taken place in apportionment methods. The text also provides background for classroom discussion on topics such as gerrymandering and the size of the House of Representatives.

We, the Americans Series. Based on 1980 census and more recent Census Bureau survey information, these booklets give sweeping profiles of the total population, women, Blacks, persons of Spanish origin, American Indian and Alaska Natives, and Asian & Pacific Islander populations. With succinct, understandable commentary and effective graphics, they look at topics such as education, income, marital status, and voting participation. The *We, the Americans* series has been designed primarily for high school students and beyond. Also, *Nosotros'* bilingual format makes it an excellent addition to ESL and Spanish language classes.

Statistical Abstract of the United States: 1989. Annual since 1878. The most comprehensive, single volume document produced by the Census Bureau. Summary data on over 30 topics-covering the demographic, social, economic, and political organization of the United States-make this an excellent reference. This edition features over 1,400 tables and graphic charts, special state rankings for 60 selected data items, and a guide to sources.

County and City Data Book: 1988. Published every 5 years. The *County and City Data Book* (over 1,000 pages) provides a comprehensive demographic, social, and economic profile for the Nation, the states (and the District of Columbia), 3,139 counties, and 945 cities with 25,000 or more inhabitants. It includes scores of data items (such as crime, population, housing, race, age, employment, land area, personal income) for the above areas, 4 data items for 10,000 incorporated places/minor civil divisions with 2,500 or more population, and maps for each state showing counties and some place locations. Rankings are provided for the top 75 cities and counties by selected characteristics.

1980 Population Distribution Map. (Also known as the *Night-time Map*.) *The Night-time Map* is one of the most popular maps produced by the Census Bureau. Population distribution is depicted across the country using white dots (one dot = 1,000 people) on a blue-black field, as if every household's "lights are on". The map shows no state boundaries or city names. Some mountain ranges and river valleys are evident because of settlement patterns.

Congressional Districts of the 100th Congress of the United States. Use this map to continue the celebration of the Bicentennial of the Constitution and to celebrate the Bicentennial of the Census of Population. This product commemorates not only the 100th Congress (January 1987-January 1989), but also the 75th, 50th, 25th, and 1st. The front of the map shows the boundaries of districts in the 100th Congress and gives students a graphic picture of equal representation. The number of Representatives by state also is displayed in tabular form. Maps for Puerto Rico and the outlying areas are shown. The reverse side shows the boundaries of the voting and nonvoting areas of the country and the district borders at the time of the 1st, 25th, 50th, 75th, and 100th Congresses. This side clearly demonstrates the geographic expansion of the country, the formation of the states, district boundary changes, and the effect of population change on representation.

NOTE: The boundaries of the districts of 101st Congress are the same as those of the 100th.

To learn more about these and other useful Census Bureau products, request a free copy of the *1990 Census Education Project* teaching kit. (Supply limited.) Ordering information for the items listed above also available.

Contact: Customer Services Branch
Data User Services Division
Bureau of the Census
Washington, DC 20233
(301) 763-4100

50

Chapter 6

Social Mathematics
H. Michael Hartoonian

Introduction

The increasing complexity of today's world is forcing social studies teachers to expand their skills and knowledge base from working with computers to understanding international monetary markets. Perhaps no other area of the curriculum is faced with the variety and magnitude of information, issues, and events as the social studies. We are even beginning to realize that the quantity and quality of information are changing the way we perceive ourselves and our Republic. In *The Geopolitics of Information*, Anthony Smith (1980, 131, 37) states:

> The whole history of the nation as a political unit of mankind has been predicated upon territoriality; the technology of printing came into being in the same era as the nation-state and both seemed to be reaching the end of their usefulness in the era of the computer; it is physically impossible to impose upon data the same kinds of controls that are imposed upon goods and paper-borne information, though the world will inevitably continue to try to do so for some [time]. ... The problem is simply that there is not room in the long run for conflicting information doctrines within a world which is becoming increasingly interconnected.

> *The quality and quantity of information are changing the way we perceive ourselves and our Republic.*

Smith's observations simply and strongly suggest that social studies teachers must give information a more central place in their instructional programs. At the heart of understanding and judging information is the need for quantitative skills or "social mathematics." Social mathematics includes abilities that are used when we measure or quantify social phenomena in any way and communicate these measures to others, plus those related abilities that we need when judging the information presented to us as we decide whom to vote for, what car to purchase, or what personal economic course to follow.

Social mathematics, as the concept is used here, includes the study and use of statistics and probability applied to the social world. Part of this definition includes methods of observation and data collection. Social mathematics helps us solve problems and make decisions in the face of uncertainties because of incomplete information. The terms 'probability' and 'chance' are applied to situations whose outcome we cannot precisely determine in advance. Most events are reported in terms of chance or probability—the chance of rain tomorrow, the probability of living to be 90, the chance of winning an election. Statistics help us to understand better such notions as GNP or inflation rates, as well as many concepts we read about in newspapers or see on television that are rooted in social mathematics. Once we have an under-

Social Mathematics

standing of probability, statistics, and some supportive concepts, we can improve the assessment of the direction and magnitude of social trends and events as we make personal and social (policy) decisions. Social mathematics, then, includes those abilities we need when doing simple computations at the grocery store or understanding the significance of a Gallup poll. Television ratings, school evaluations, voting trends, employment, and inflation rates are all examples of social mathematics in everyday life, and if citizens are to be literate, knowledge of such ideas as mode, mean, sample, population, randomness, and probability is necessary. Statistical concepts are so commonly used and abused in newspapers, on television, and by politicians or business persons to communicate data that citizens without these abilities are intellectually, politically, legally, and economically at risk.

Quantitative Concepts

Let us begin with some definitions of quantitative concepts that can serve as a foundation for social mathematics. The ideas below are necessary to our understanding of data and their use in social studies, and the reader is encouraged to investigate and learn more about each term than is provided here.

Statistical concepts are commonly used and abused in newspapers.

Statistics and probability are involved when we collect, organize, analyze, and use data in simulations or real life. Statistics is the theory and method of analyzing data to study and compare underlying patterns and relationships to accept or reject hypotheses and to aid in making decisions about empirical observations. A statistic is a measure calculated from the whole population of data or a sample* of data within a population.

Probability is the estimate of the likelihood of an event's occurrence. In measurement, predictions are made in terms of probability statements, such as, the chances are 99 in 100 that such an event will occur. Stated another way, we can say that probability deals with the question of how we can, within a sample space, determine the successful outcomes from the total possible outcomes. A major-league baseball player who gets three hits (successful outcomes) in ten times at bat (total possible outcomes) has a batting average of .300 or 30 percent.

From these data, we can say that, on average, this player gets about one hit every three times he comes up to bat. It does not tell us, however, that he will get a hit once every three times he comes to bat.

*Sampling is the process of drawing a set of items from a population. A random sample is a sample so drawn that every individual in the population has an equal chance of being drawn into it. Random sampling is basic to the use of sampling statistics, that branch of statistics concerned with making inferences about population values based upon the value of a subpopulation or smaller population.

One of the quantitative concepts used in social mathematics is *ratio*. Probabilities are often expressed in ratios. Along with percent and index number, they are fundamental ways in which statistics are reported. A ratio is a relation of degree or number. It is a relative amount. It is the relation between two numbers or two magnitudes of the same kind; especially the quotient of one magnitude divided by the other, or the factor that, multiplied by one, will produce the other. Ratio and proportion are related in that x/y is a ratio, whereas x/y = a/b is a proportion. A country's well-being might be expressed, for example, in a ratio, GNP/Population; whereas the relationship between money supply, its circulation, and prices, and the total goods and services produced is a proportional notion.

Percent is an amount or quantity commensurate with a number of units in proportion to 100: For example; 50 percent of the people means one half of the population; 50 percent of 100 is 50. A percent is a ratio based on 100.

An *index number* is any of a series of numbers indicating the quantitative changes in a given statistical aggregate over time, such as prices, costs, and so forth. Index numbers have a reference number or arbitrary base (usually 100) which represents the status of the aggregate at a specific previous time or period. For example, farm prices are at 80 percent of parity. This means that farm prices are at 80 percent of a given base year. Cost of living figures are another example of index numbers.

> √ *Ratio*
> √ *Percent*
> √ *Index number*
> √ *Central tendency*
> √ *Dispersion*
> √ *Mean*
> √ *Median*
> √ *Mode*
> √ *Range*

We often use measures of *central tendency* and *dispersion* to represent large quantities of data. The three measures of central tendency are mean, median, and mode. Three measures are needed because of the characteristics of the distribution of scores, items, or events under study. For example, if all distributions of scores were normal, then we would need only one measure. But almost all distributions are not normal so we must be able to use any or all of the three measures to get a fair picture of the population or sample that we are observing.

The *mean* score is the sum of the raw scores divided by the number of cases. Mean is also called average. For example, the raw scores of 2, 3, 4, 5, and 6 have a total of 2 + 3 + 4 + 5 + 6 = 20; if you divide 20 by 5 (the number of cases) you arrive at the mean (4).

The *median* is that point in a distribution of scores with 50 percent of the cases on each side of it, the midpoint of a distribution. For example, in the distribution 2, 4, 6, 8, and 10, the median is 6.

The *mode* is that score which appears most frequently in a set of scores. When scores are arranged in a frequency distribution, the mode is taken to be the midpoint of the interval containing the largest number of cases. Mode is the least frequently used measure of central tendency. For example, in the set of scores, 2, 4, 6, 8, 8, 8, 6, 4, and 2, the mode is 8.

Social Mathematics

In addition to measures of central tendency, there are issues and measures of dispersion like range and standard deviation. These concepts are also important in reporting statistics.

Statistics are also generated, organized, and analyzed in simulations. Computer simulations can allow us to study large populations with great speed and can help us design graphs and charts to display and use the data. Simulations enable us to study problems that we might not be able to conduct in the real world.

Social Mathematics and Social Studies Curriculum

> *It is extremely important that social studies teachers work with members of the mathematics faculty.*

With regard to the social studies curriculum and social mathematics, it is extremely important that social studies teachers work with members of the mathematics faculty in their school to determine where and how statistics and probability should be taught in the K–12 mathematics and social studies programs. This information will help in the process of sequence development for the social studies curriculum, and mathematics teachers may already be aware of the importance of quantitative concepts in the school program. The National Council of Teachers of Mathematics (NCTM) in its *Agenda for Action* (1981) recommended that the curriculum for the 1980s and beyond include "locating and processing quantitative information; collecting data; organizing and presenting data; interpreting data; drawing inferences; and predicting from data."

A Good Time for Collaboration

(Social Studies teacher: "We need some support in getting started with social data processing on computers." Math teacher: "We need some real-life numbers to use in our problems.")

The National Science Board Committee on Precollege Education in Mathematics, Science, and Technology (CBMS 1982) stated that the elementary schools should provide "basic understanding of data analysis, simple statistics and probability...and that...elementary statistics and probability should now be considered fundamental for all high school students." In 1987 the National Council of Teachers of Mathematics stated that the application of mathematics to the social sciences has never been greater (NCTM 1987).

Within the mathematics education community, these statements are typical. Schools are being asked to help students cope effectively with the vast amounts of data they will encounter in almost every facet of their lives. Thus statistics, the study of data, is becoming a more vital component of mathematics instruction. The same must hold true of the social studies.

The social studies can support the mathematics curriculum in the common goal of teaching and learning statistics and probability. For example, within the K–12 program, consider team-planning and team-teaching the following social mathematic objectives adapted from *A Guide to Curriculum Planning in Mathematics* (1986):

K–3

*Explore the concept of chance, based upon repeated observations of real world events such as weather, games, or contests.

*Gather data by counting, by performing simple experiments, by measuring, or from various media sources such as newspapers, almanacs, and magazines.

*Organize a set of data by tallying and ordering.

*Construct bar graphs and pictograms. State impressions obtained from these graphs. The data for these visual displays should come from problems or situations that occur within the classroom or in the community.

4–6

*Explore the importance of statistics in society through citing their use in newspapers, magazines, and television.

*Become familiar with the use of numbers and graphs in newspapers, magazines, and television, and other sources within society.

*Using a graphic presentation of a set of data, recognize and describe patterns such as increases, decreases, or trends.

| Social Mathematics |

These objectives fit well into a general social studies curriculum pattern.

*Explore the concept of probability by working with simple models such as dice and coins and also by conducting sample experiments to make probability predictions at home, at school, and in the community.

*Explore different kinds of data generated by others and evaluate the sources of those data. Recognize that bias in a question can affect results or interpretations of those data.

*Gather data by conducting a survey or by carrying out a simulation.

7–8

*Become familiar with the United States census. Know how the census is given, when it is given, what kinds of questions are contained in the census, why the census is given, and what uses are made of the information gathered.

*Explore concepts of independent, dependent, and mutually exclusive events.

*Compare the odds for or against a given event.

*Construct scatter plots, circle graphs, frequency polygons, and box plots. State impressions obtained from these graphs.

*Distinguish between a survey (sample) and a census (population), and understand when each is necessary, why a survey might be given, and by whom.

9–12

*Apply the methods of statistics to study trends and situations drawn from such fields as politics, advertising, medicine, business, industry, and science. The question of the role of ethics in the application of statistics should also be addressed.

*Recognize the use and misuse of statistics in newspapers, magazines, texts, television, and other sources in society.

*Recognize valid and invalid reasoning. Evaluation should be made of statistical arguments found in newspapers, on television, in magazines, and other sources relevant to the student.

*Express conclusions and interpretations in written form for a given presentation of data. The ability to communicate clearly the results of an analysis of a set of data should be considered a part of the procedure.

*Select an appropriate sampling method for a given experiment.

*Estimate population parameters from sample statistics.

These objectives can fit nicely into a general social studies curriculum pattern. Each set of objectives K–3, 4–6, 7–8, and 9–12 can be used in this general pattern from which the curriculum committee, made up of social studies and mathematics teachers, can go on to develop content, plan activities, and gather resources.

Start with a joint K–12 social studies/ mathematics curriculum committee.

The major curricular tasks are to identify and incorporate social mathematics *objectives* and *content* into the social studies scope and sequence. In other words, social mathematics needs a curricular home, and although social studies educators can play a major role in designing this home, we still need help from mathematics educators in its construction.

Curriculum development efforts might start, then, with a joint K–12 social studies/mathematics committee to review the two content areas and determine where social mathematics objectives such as those listed above might best be implemented. Once such a determination is made, attention must be given to materials and staff development needs. It may well be the case that individuals already on staff, e.g., librarians, mathematics faculty members, supervisors, and, of course, social studies teachers, can provide in-service and consultant help in this effort. The major goal of this curriculum committee is to develop a scope and sequence design that shows what social mathematics content is to be taught in the K–12 social studies program and how this content is to be supplemented, enriched, and correlated with the K–12 mathematics curriculum.

Social Mathematics and Social Studies Instruction

Instructional strategies for teaching social mathematics are similar to those we use in the general mathematics or social studies programs. However, teachers should focus on two important goals. First, we should try to address directly such major concepts as probability, ratio, index number, central tendency, and sampling. Second, we should try to use these concepts with teaching strategies that allow students many opportunities for hands-on activities. For example, within a unit on community (social) institutions, students studying the institution of education might develop a graph of the number or percent of people in their community or in three different world communities that have an elementary, high school, or college education. Using numbers can be enjoyable and an important part of any social study, particularly when we want to compare and contrast social phenomena.

There follows a series of general K–12 social mathematics strategies that can help the curriculum committee generate ideas for the instructional program.

K–3

At the primary grades, pictorial graphing can be used to help children relate or compare a number of things. For example, students who walk, ride the bus, or are driven to school can be pictorially described. Students can also see this distribution change each month and discuss why. Other graphing ideas can involve birthdays (month or date of month), height, shoe size, number of pets, size of family, and so forth.

A favorite activity of children that can aid in pictorial graphing is called two-dice adding. After two dice are thrown, their sum is calculated and the appropriate square on the graph, below, is colored to indicate the sum. The activity can be played by two children or two teams of children. The object of the activity is to see the distribution of sums on each child's or team's graph. Students can guess what would happen if they play the game again.

The Two-Dice Race

2	3	4	5	6	7	8	9	10	11	12

Children also like to guess how many things they can do within a certain period of time. An egg timer can help children study time by asking them to predict how often an event will occur within a certain time. How many ring tosses can be made on a soft-drink bottle in one minute? How many times can you write your name in thirty seconds? How many stores or churches can you see and count in a picture of a town in one minute?

Children also like to predict or form hypotheses about the future. For example, how many students will be absent next week? How would you predict your answer? How would you test your hunch?

A good introduction to the concept of probability is to have children consider the following events and state how likely each is to occur. Place a line on the board and at one end of the line write 'impossible' and on the other end write 'certain'. Have students place a letter on the line as an indicator of how certain or impossible they believe each event to be.

Impossible_____/_____/_____/_____/_____/_____Certain
    A. I will be in school tomorrow.
    B. It will snow in our town in June.
    C. Next year there will be more boys than girls in my class.
    D. I will graduate from college.
    E. Next Sunday we will visit friends in another city.

Discuss why they placed the letter where they did, and help them conceptualize the notion of chance. Discuss why some events are more likely while others are less likely to happen.

4–6

At the intermediate grades, social studies and mathematics teachers working together can incorporate the skills of statistics and probability into the content of the social studies program. The social studies can provide excellent applications for the concepts and skills learned within the mathematics program.

Within the 4–6 curriculum, students can deal with state, regional, and national data from popular songs and movies to state and national election trends. For example, student interviews (the interviewed students should be randomly selected from all students in the school) can be conducted on the popularity of certain political candidates, movies, or cafeteria food. From these data, estimates on elections, percentages of students who saw movie X, or the number of students who eat in the cafeteria on certain days can be obtained. Students can discuss how these data can be used to help cooks plan the week's meals.

At these grade levels, it is also important to help students think about the numbers of activities in which they are engaged that demand quantitative skills. Ask students to keep a log on such activities (i.e., making a purchase, figuring batting averages, and reading graphs in textbooks or newspapers.

Social Mathematics

7–8

Middle school students can begin to deal more directly with social statistics. For example, students can conduct a study to see which classmates lived in the state all their lives, who recently (within five years) moved into the state, and which other states and countries are represented. From these data, students can predict trends of in-migration and the probability of the school's population makeup in the future. That is, they can estimate the probability that a new student will be from other states or other countries (and which countries). Students can also study and graphically portray the amount of trade from their state or from the United States to various parts of the world and make estimates of its growth or decline.

9–12

At the high school level, students can engage social mathematics to analyze how statistical data are used and misused in public debates as well as to communicate numerical information precisely in personal arguments and classroom presentations. On the former point, students can keep a log of the misuses of statistics that they see in newspapers, journals, advertisements, and on television. From biased samples to misuses of percent data, there are many instances in which citizens must be aware of data manipulation by special-interest groups.

Students can also prepare data displays of the television viewing habits of their high school based upon a random sample (for example, ten percent) of the student body. They can compare and contrast this data display with a similar display of viewing habits of the teachers or parents using the same sampling procedures. They might also use want ads of a city newspaper and prepare a data display of

1. Types and numbers of jobs available on particular days
2. The percent change of jobs in one category in relationship to other categories over a given period of time

Students can use social statistics to make regional comparisons on such topics as life expectancy. Sample questions based on the data in the margin are these:

1. Which nation in Europe had the highest life expectancy in 1986? _____ Which had the lowest? _____
2. What was the mean, median, and mode of life expectancy in Europe in 1986? Mean ____; Median_____; Mode_____.
3. What was the mean, median, and mode of life expectancy in South America in 1986? Mean ____; Median_____; Mode_____.

Life Expectancy Europe 1986

Albania	69
Austria	73
Belgium	73
Bulgaria	72
Cyprus	74
Czechoslovakia	72
Denmark	75
Finland	73
France	75
Germany (East)	73
Germany (West)	73
Greece	74
Hungary	71
Iceland	77
Ireland	73
Italy	73
Luxembourg	73
Malta	73
Netherlands	76
Norway	76
Poland	72
Portugal	73
Romania	71
Spain	74
Sweden	76
Switzerland	76
USSR	71
United Kingdom	71
Yugoslavia	71

4. Make a frequency-distribution chart of life expectancy in Europe and South America. Place a check (√) at the appropriate place on the chart for each nation. Compare the two continents.

Europe

80 yrs	75 yrs	70 yrs	65 yrs	60 yrs	55 yrs	50 yrs	45 yrs

South America

80 yrs	75 yrs	70 yrs	65 yrs	60 yrs	55 yrs	50 yrs	45 yrs

Life Expectancy South America 1986

Argentina	68
Bolivia	49
Brazil	63
Chile	67
Colombia	65
Ecuador	64
Guyana	70
Paraguay	68
Peru	60
Suriname	69
Uruguay	70
Venezuela	68

5. On a blank outline map of Europe, color in four regions of life expectancy. For example, nations with over 75 years of life expectancy could be the top region. Make a key to show your cutoff points. Do the same for South America.

In most high school social studies courses, computer software exists that can help teachers generate, organize, and analyze these kinds of data. The computer can be a great source of random data generation. The computer is of particular importance when dealing with large data bases like the United States census. Through computer analysis, students can see better the variability of experimental and survey results from group to group. This can be a basis for discussion of sources of bias in the data-gathering process. It can also help in showing how the size of a sample may influence experimental results.

To help social studies teachers generate instructional ideas, it might be useful to look at the new publications on data gathering and probability that the

Social Mathematics

National Council of Teachers of Mathematics and the National Science Foundation have recently developed. Your colleagues in the mathematics department probably already have copies of these materials.

> *Understanding number data in all their uses and misuses is a must for citizens of the Republic.*

The numbers are coming! The numbers are coming!

Conclusion

Three major topics addressed here—rationale for social mathematics, curriculum design, and instructional strategies—are attempts to bring the numerical side of social studies into a more central position within our field and put social mathematics higher on the professional agenda of social studies teachers. This is consistent, of course, with research and literature in the several social science disciplines, and it is a simple truth of late 20th-century life that understanding number data in all their various uses and misuses is a must for citizens of the Republic.

62

References

A Guide to Curriculum Planning in Mathematics. Madison, Wisconsin: Wisconsin Department of Public Instruction, 1986.

Cathcart, G., and J. Kirkpatrick, eds. *Organizing Data and Dealing with Uncertainty*. Reston, Virginia: National Council of Teachers of Mathematics, 1979.

Gawronski, J.D., and D.B. MacLeod. "Probability and Statistics: Today's Ciphering?" In *Selected Issues in Mathematics Education*, ed. M.M. Lindquist. Berkeley, California: McCutchan Publishing Corporation, 1980.

Hardyck, C., and L. Petrinovich. *Understanding Research in the Social Sciences: A Practical Guide to Social and Behavioral Research*. Philadelphia: W.B. Saunders, 1975.

The Conference Board of Mathematical Sciences. *The Mathematical Sciences Curriculum K–12: What Is Still Fundamental and What Is Not*. Washington, D.C.: National Science Foundation, 1982.

National Council of Teachers of Mathematics (NCTM). *An Agenda for Action*. Reston, Virginia: Recommendations for School Mathematics of the 1980s, 1981.

National Council of Teachers of Mathematics. *Teaching Statistics and Probability Yearbook*. Reston, Virginia: National Council of Teachers of Mathematics, 1980.

National Council of Teachers of Mathematics. *Curriculum and Evaluation Standards for School Mathematics*. Reston, Virginia: National Council of Teachers of Mathematics, 1987.

Newman, C., T.E. Obrenski, and R.L. Schaeffer. *Introduction to Probability*. Palo Alto, California: Dale Seymour Publications, 1986.

Smith, A. *The Geopolitics of Information*. New York: Oxford University Press, 1980.

Tanur, J., et al. *Statistics: A Guide to Business and Economics*. San Francisco: Holden-Day, 1976.

Social Mathematics

Essential resources for any social mathematics program:

Statistical Abstract of the United States (Annual). Washington, D.C.: United States Department of Commerce, Bureau of the Census.

Historical Statistics of the United States. Washington, D.C.: United States Department of Commerce, Bureau of the Census, 1975.

Both are for sale from the Superintendent of Documents, U.S. Government Printing Office, Washington, D.C., 20402. Telephone: (202) 783-3238.

Chapter 7

Tools for Social Mathematics
James G. Lengel

Social studies are hardly ever mathematical, and mathematics is seldom social. Especially in elementary and secondary schools, the tools of mathematics remain cumbersome and for many students impossible to use in social studies classes. To carry out by hand the turbid calculations necessary to quantify most meaningful social phenomena is beyond the patience and attention span of most students (and most teachers as well). By the time the detailed arithmetic is completed, students have forgotten what the social issue was.

A few social studies teachers, with great planning and forbearance, have managed to overcome the mathematical bottleneck and bring quantity to bear on the social studies. But they remain a minority.

They need not remain so for long. The newest crop of small computers with their easy-to-use software can do the drudge arithmetic calculations, allowing teachers and students to consider issues and think about the implications. Until now, there have been too few computers (one for every 30 students is not enough), located in the wrong place, and loaded with software whose arcane threads only a mathematical Theseus could unravel. It is no wonder that the computer has neither revolutionized the teaching of social studies nor delivered the magic of mathematics to our field.

Michael Hartoonian is more than correct when he points out the need for teachers and students to be more mathematical. We can no longer make sense of an information-rich world without understanding mathematics concepts and without the ability to apply those concepts to the data we see, teach, and learn every day. For most of us, the pain we endure through the calculations and machinations are not worth the reward. Computers can ease the pain if we learn to use a few of their simple tools.

The remainder of this article shows how microcomputers can be used to help with the mathematics for each of the examples in Michael Hartoonian's chapter. Note that, in each example, the computer neither solves the problem nor provides the answer. Instead, it helps us do so by performing the calculations and keeping the records for us. Note also that the computer tools used—mostly spreadsheets—are widely accessible and operable even by primary-grade students.

> *The newest crop of small computers ... can do the drudge arithmetic calculations, allowing students to consider issues and think about implications.*

In the Early Grades

Explore the concept of chance in this social studies lesson: Spin a globe. Close your eyes and stop the globe with your finger. Where is your finger

Tools for Social Mathematics

when it stops? Record the name of the continent it lands on (or the ocean). Ask students to predict, if we spin and point several dozen times in a row, which continents would record the most "hits." Then proceed to spin and point 24 times, recording the "hit" each time. Keep the records on a spreadsheet prepared in advance that looks like Figure 1:

Figure 1. Record of "Hits"

	A	B	C	D	E	F	G	H	I	J	K	L	M	N	O	P	Q	R	S	T	U	V	W	X	Y	Z
1	Continent																									Total
2																										
3	Asia							1					1						1			1				4
4	Africa	1					1				1															3
5	Australia				1								1													2
6	North America		1													1								1		3
7	South America									1						1										2
8	Europe					1					1										1					3
9	Antarctica																									0
10	Ocean	1		1				1	1					1				1		1						7
11																										
12																										24

If you set up a formula beforehand in the rightmost column, the spreadsheet will keep a running total for each continent. When you have completed all the spins, look at the totals and compare them against the students' predictions. You might wish to sort the continents by frequency of hits, to make the relationships easier to see, like this:

Figure 2. Continent "Hits" in Rank Order

	A	B	C	D	E	F	G	H	I	J	K	L	M	N	O	P	Q	R	S	T	U	V	W	X	Y	Z
14	Continent																									Total
15																										
16	Antarctica																									0
17	Australia				1								1													2
18	South America									1						1										2
19	Africa	1					1				1															3
20	North America		1													1								1		3
21	Europe					1					1										1					3
22	Asia							1					1						1			1				4
23	Ocean	1		1				1	1					1				1		1						7
24																										
25																										24

Take the lesson further by graphing the totals, to show students the relationship between the continents in a more direct visual manner as illustrated in Figure 3.

Finally, ask what would happen if we erased the spreadsheet and repeated the 24 spins. Would the graph look the same? Through this lesson, students learn not only about the layout of the earth, but also about chance and data analysis.

Figure 3. Graph of Continents

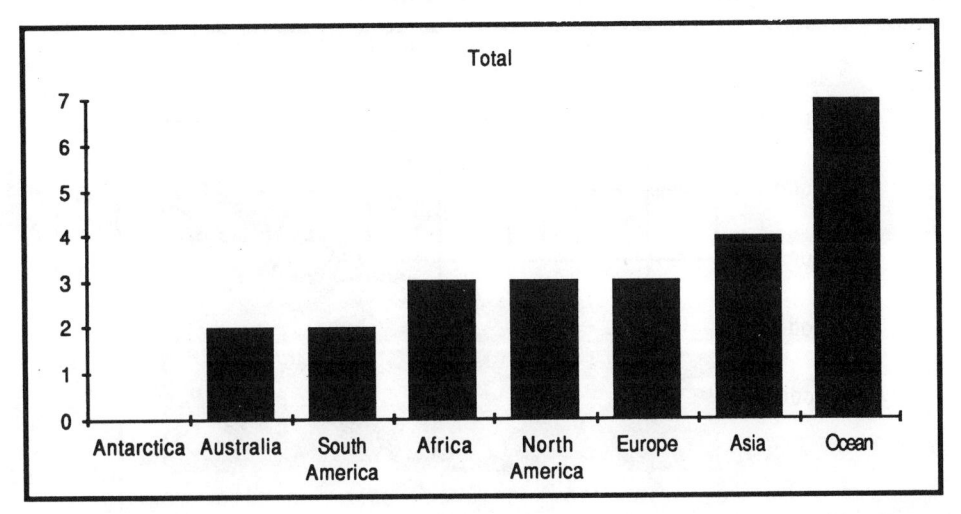

[Bar chart titled "Total" showing values: Antarctica 0, Australia 2, South America 2, Africa 3, North America 3, Europe 3, Asia 4, Ocean 7]

The same spreadsheet tool, set up in a similar fashion, can be used to record and analyze data from other social experiments and collections. These kinds of lessons practice the mathematical arts of predicting results, recording measurements, finding sums, sorting and reorganizing data, and turning numbers into a graph. They also practice the social studies skills of drawing conclusions from data, and relating numbers to real things.

A spreadsheet like the one used to produce these examples requires no computer programming skills. You simply type the numbers into the rows, and choose mathematical functions by pointing to them on a list. Turning a table of numbers into a graph is automatic as well, requiring only three or four keystrokes or mouse clicks. The results, whether mathematical or graphical, appear instantly on the screen. Printing the results calls for two keystrokes or mouse clicks.

A spreadsheet ... requires no programming skills.

In the Later Grades

Using again the spreadsheet as a mathematical tool, try this lesson. Find a table of data in today's newspaper. It could be anything from weather reports to sports scores to imports and exports. Historical or time-series data are especially well-suited to this lesson. Record the data on a spreadsheet, like Figure 4.

Figure 4. Population of the United States

Year			
1900	76,212,168	1950	151,325,798
1910	92,228,496	1960	179,323,175
1920	106,021,537	1970	203,302,031
1930	123,202,624	1980	226,547,082
1940	132,164,569		

Tools for Social Mathematics

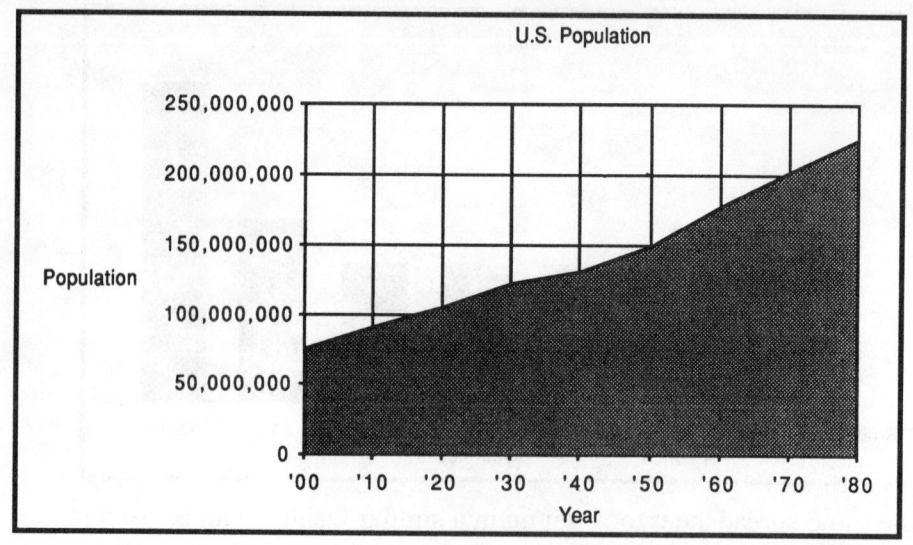

The computer very quickly performs the manual skills of arithmetic calculation.

Figure 5. United States Population

Ask students what type of graph would best display these data visually. Discuss the effects of the various types of graphs (bar, pie, column, area, line, scatter, picture, etc.). Now create several graphs from the spreadsheet, and ask students which type appears best at making the relationships clear. For example, Figure 5 shows the information in a line graph. Discuss the content of the graphs, with students drawing conclusions from the table and the graphs. Did they find it easier to draw conclusions from the table of numbers, or from one of the graphs?

Figure 6. United States Population Projection

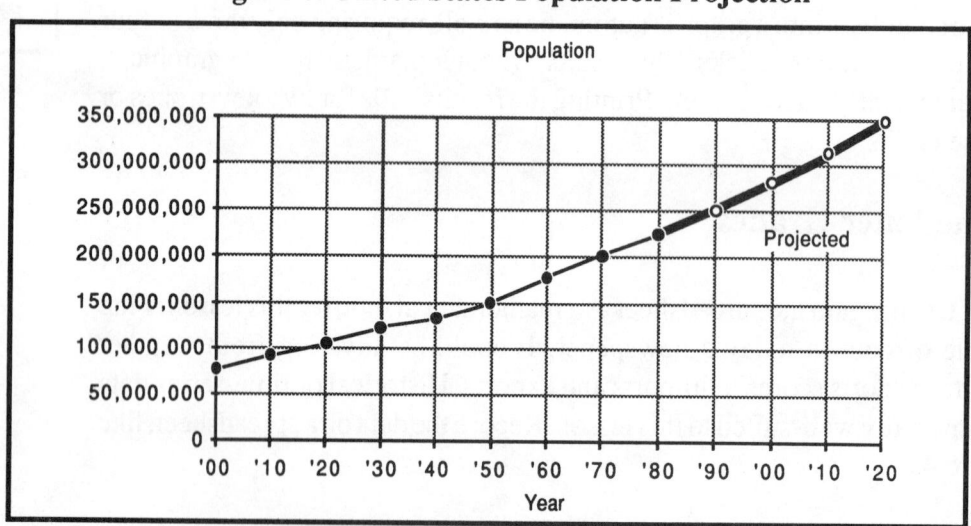

The second part of this lesson reverses the process—students find a chart in the newspaper or in their textbook, and enter it into the spreadsheet as a table of numbers. Use the spreadsheet tools to reorganize the table, find sums and averages, or to extrapolate trends as shown in Figure 6.

Then turn this table back into a graph, using the computer's instant graphing tools. Display the same data as a different kind of graph.

Tools for Social Mathematics

The Role of the Computer

In both these lessons, the computer very quickly performs the manual chores of arithmetic computation, rewriting data in a different order, and plotting points into graphs. Without the computer, these tasks would probably take longer than a class period and result in many lost "teachable moments." Note, however, that the computer does not do the intellectual work here—that is the responsibility of the students. The computer does *not* draw conclusions or find meaning in data. But the speed of the computer in these lessons allows the students time and occasion to see meaning in the data and to apply their intellects to them.

The computer does not draw conclusions or find meaning in data. That is left to the students.

Nor in these lessons does the computer *teach*. It provides no direct instruction to students. But the computer certainly helps the teacher to teach and the student to learn. Isn't that its proper place?

Note also that the students and teacher are learning in a group. These are not solitary exercises. They are not private interactions between an individual and a computer screen. Students discuss, argue, try things out, reformat what they find, ask new questions, and work as a group to explore the issues at hand. Both content and process are social. For these kinds of lessons, it is better to employ a few computers in the regular classroom than to traipse down to the computer lab and have each student work alone behind a machine.

More Lesson Ideas

The school offers myriad opportunities for students to collect and analyze social data. Here are some more examples of lessons that could be constructed around the spreadsheet as a recording and analysis tool.

√ Obtain from the cafeteria manager the number of hot lunches sold each day, along with the menu. Record the results over a month on a spreadsheet. Sort the data by day of week and type of food, looking for trends and patterns. Graphing the data may also allow you to see more easily any relationships that exist rather than by looking only at the numbers. Discuss the findings, and then use the word-processing tools of the computer to develop a presentation (complete with tables and graphs) to the cafeteria manager on the findings.

For these kinds of lessons, it is better to employ a few computers in the regular classroom than to traipse down to the computer lab.

√ Obtain from the school office the attendance totals (by class, if possible) each day for a month. Record them on the spreadsheet, along with the day's weather and temperature. Use the sorting and graphing capabilities of the spreadsheet to look for trends and patterns. Discuss the findings (what might be some possible causes of the trends found?), draw conclusions, and then use the word processor to prepare a report to communicate the results to the principal.

| Tools for Social Mathematics |

> *Nor in these lessons does the computer teach. But the computer certainly helps the teacher to teach and the students to learn. Isn't that its proper place?*

√ Record each day the readings from the school's electric or gas meter. Record also the day's average temperature, taken from the local newspaper or your own thermometer.

√ Dial CompuServe or other source from your computer. (Many school libraries are all set up to access dial-up information services such as this. Ask your school librarian for assistance.) Go to the demographics section, and choose CENDATA, the source for on-line U.S. Census data. Download a few tables of data on a topic of relevance to your course work. Read the table into the spreadsheet. Use the sorting, summing, averaging, and graphing tools in the spreadsheet to explore trends and patterns in the data. Discuss the meaning of your findings. Develop a report on the word processor, with accompanying graphs and tables (clipped directly from the spreadsheet), to communicate the results.

Any and all of the surveys and data collections described in the second half of Hartoonian's chapter can benefit from the application of a computer, in most cases to record, analyze, and graph the results.

All these lessons can be enhanced if teachers ask students to predict in advance what they think the data will show. Halfway along in the data collection, ask students whether they wish to modify their predictions. At the end of the lesson, ask them to explain any discrepancies between their predictions and the final outcome.

Through these kinds of lessons, students will enhance not only their knowledge of the social topics and issues at hand, but also develop their ability to think quantitatively about social data. Finally, these lessons develop in them a facility with common information tools such as the spreadsheet and data-base searching. These tools enable students to understand and find new meanings in the world around them.

Chapter 8

Social Problem Solving Using Data Bases
Norris M. Sanders

In the Industrial Revolution, the introduction of mechanical tools extended the power and precision of a worker's hands. Can the computer extend the power and precision of a worker's (student's) brain in the Information Age?

This chapter will address these questions:
1. What are the common features of data-base programs? Give examples of how they are used.
2. What classroom equipment and software are necessary for serious data processing?
3. How can social data processing be built into the curriculum?
4. What training do teachers need to lead a class in data processing?

> *Can the computer extend the power and precision of a student's brain?*

1. What are the common features of data-base programs?

Data processing involves two elements:
- a reservoir of information on a computer disk or tape
- a computer program that processes the information

Processing information means selecting designated data from the reservoir and sorting it in a manner useful to the operator. If the information is numerical the program can perform mathematical calculations. Some programs process information into a variety of maps and graphs. The operator of the data base uses the keyboard or a mouse to choose which information to address and which processes to activate. Most often this involves selecting items from a simple multiple-choice menu.

Hail to the Chief is an entry level data base containing information on U.S. presidents. For data, it provides 10 characteristics of each president as shown in the following example for Thomas Jefferson.

```
NAME: Jefferson, Thomas
PRESIDENT NUMBER: 3
PRIOR POLITICAL EXPERIENCE: Governor, Cabinet, Vice Pres.
PRIOR PROFESSION: Law, Politics
POLITICAL PARTY: Democratic-Republican
% MILITARY EXPENSES: 49
SUPREME COURT APPOINTMENTS: 3
BILLS PASSED: 351
VETOES DURING TERM: 0
COUNTRY AT PEACE: Yes
```

Social Problem Solving Using a Data Base

The student can call to the screen the information necessary to answer such questions as the following:
1. Which presidents did not veto any bills?
2. Rank-order the presidents in terms of the number of vetoes exercised.
3. How many presidents had no wars during their terms?

Entry-level programs do not have much problem-solving power but they are useful in demonstrating the nature of data processing to intermediate grade or junior high students. Students often realize that they could answer the same questions easily from a chart and would not have to bother with the computer. Many home applications, such as keeping a list of books in a personal library or recipes or a Christmas card list, are not time-saving if you consider the effort necessary to set up the data base in the first place. Data bases are indispensable when there is a mass of information, as in the case of a grocer checking inventory or a librarian keeping track of books. The same advantages are found in the more sophisticated social studies programs.

> *Data bases are indispensable when there is a mass of information.*

Data base programs can be roughly classified into four groups:

- "Entry-level programs" contain a few processing functions and a small amount of information plus the capacity to receive additional data. Examples are *Friendly Filer* and *Create-a-Base*. These programs mainly search and sort. Some have a simple spreadsheet.

- "Omnibus programs" have little or no information but have more processing functions than the entry programs. These normally can make a functional spreadsheet and some have graphing functions or word processing to write a report. Omnibus programs can be used in many school subjects, at home, or in a small business. They accommodate a large amount of information but users must insert their own records. Examples are *Appleworks*; *pfs File, Report and Graph*; and *Bank Street Filer*.

- "Piggyback programs" contain large amounts of information on some subjects but no processing tools. These programs are to be used with one of the data processing programs listed in the previous category. An example is *Scholastic pfs: World Geography, Cultures, and Economic Data Bases*.

- "Full featured programs" have both abundant social information plus functions to process it. An example is *The Social Studies Tool Kit*.

Each of the four categories of data-base programs has strengths and weaknesses. The entry-level programs are easy to learn These progams are good for tabulating data from an opinion poll or a student survey. Limitations are the small amount of information they can manage plus lack of processing tools. The omnibus programs have much more processing power and can accommodate abundant data. A program such as *Appleworks*s can make elaborate spreadsheets as will be demonstrated shortly and even includes a word processor to write interpretive reports. A disadvantage is that this kind of program takes considerable time to learn. Also, the user must insert the data to be processed and this can be time-consuming. Consider typing in the life expectancy for over 150 nations. In a study of nations in the 6th and 7th grades or in secondary world geography, the class would need many similar files of information to permit serious comparisons of nations.

The piggyback programs solve the problem of providing sufficient data on a particular subject but they require the additional purchase and learning of one of the omnibus programs. Finally, the full-featured programs provide processing functions and information. The *Social Studies Tool Kit* has graphing and mapping functions and it computes, correlates, and makes weighted averages. This program is easier to learn than *Appleworks* or *pfs File and Report*. A sample project is presented later in this chapter.

A Project Using *Appleworks*. *The Statistical Abstract of the United States* is packed with data related to the social studies concepts that are highlighted in curriculum bulletins and textbooks. Suppose a secondary school class in sociology is studying a unit on the family. Among other things, the textbook describes common family disruptions in the 1980s. The teacher or a student enters into *Appleworks* a file of the number of divorces in each state in 1986. For good measure, the number of marriages is also entered.

The teacher has questions like the following in mind:
1. Does the divorce rate vary significantly from state to state?
2. Does divorce occur more commonly in states with high per capita income?
3. Is the divorce rate related to the level of education of the population?

(Questions 2 and 3 are beginning investigations of cause and effect.)

Using *Appleworks*, a spreadsheet is generated as shown in Figure 1. Only the portion for the New England states is shown.

Information Age Quotation

Just as the possession of basic literacy once marked a significant dividing line in society, between the powerful and the powerless ... so numeracy is now the basic skill that increasingly establishes a status boundary in the world of work. —Patricia Cline Cohen, *A Calculating People* (Chicago: University of Chicago Press, 1982), 6.

Social Problem Solving Using a Data Base

Figure 1. *Appleworks* **Spreadsheet**

A	B	C	D	E	F	G	H	I
States	Division	Region	Marriages (1000's)	Divorces (1000's)	Pop > 18yrs (1000's)	Marriages /1000 pop over 18	Divorces /1000 pop over 18	Marriages per Divorce
NEW JERSEY	MIDDLE ATLANTIC	NORTHEAST	60.8	28.4	5812.0	10.5	4.9	2.1
NEW YORK	MIDDLE ATLANTIC	NORTHEAST	176.9	59.5	13406.0	13.2	4.4	3.0
PENNSYLVANIA	MIDDLE ATLANTIC	NORTHEAST	88.2	40.1	9041.0	9.8	4.4	2.2
		Total	325.9	128.0	28259.0	11.5	4.5	2.5
CONNECTICUT	NEW ENGLAND	NORTHEAST	26.3	9.2	2440.0	10.8	3.8	2.9
MAINE	NEW ENGLAND	NORTHEAST	12.1	5.6	874.0	13.8	6.4	2.2
MASSACHUSETTS	NEW ENGLAND	NORTHEAST	40.7	20.0	4497.0	9.1	4.4	2.0
NEW HAMPSHIRE	NEW ENGLAND	NORTHEAST	11.7	4.7	1027.0	11.4	4.6	2.5
RHODE ISLAND	NEW ENGLAND	NORTHEAST	8.0	3.7	750.0	10.7	4.9	2.2
VERMONT	NEW ENGLAND	NORTHEAST	5.6	2.4	402.0	13.9	6.0	2.3
		Total	104.4	45.6	9990.0	10.5	4.6	2.3
		Regional Total	430.3	173.6	38249.0	11.2	4.5	2.5

The number of divorces is shown in column E and the marriages in column D. New Jersey, for example, had 60,800 marriages in 1986 and 28,400 divorces. New York had almost three times as many divorces but this reflects a larger population rather than a higher divorce rate. The teacher already has the number of people over 18 years of age in every state in the data base and commands the program to create a new column labeled "Divorces per Thousand Population over 18 Years." This new column shows that the divorce rate varies considerably among New England states. Using a program entitled *TimeOut Graph,* a bar graph is created as shown in Figure 2. Information transfers automatically from *Appleworks* so no more data entry is required. A half dozen different forms of graphs can be drawn automatically with this program.

Figure 2. New England Divorce and Marriage Rates

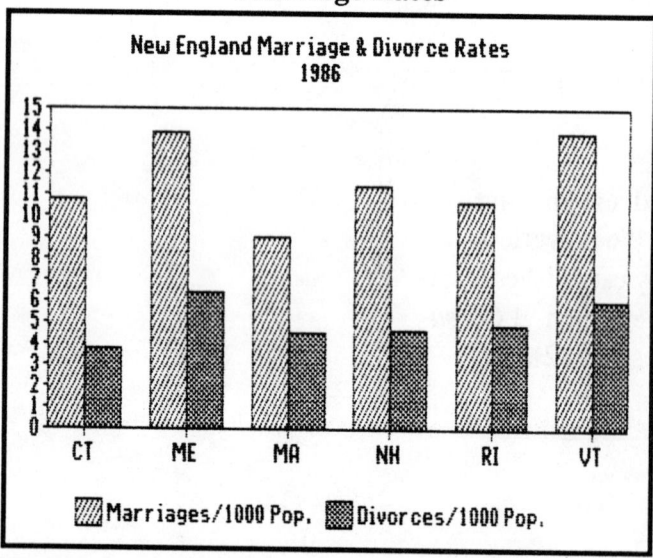

Spreadsheets with graphing features are widely used in business and are renowned for solving "what if" problems. Social scientists can also use spreadsheets. Imagine a spreadsheet on all nations of the world in column A. In column B is the

1989 population and in the column C the annual percentage growth rate. *What will the population be in each nation in the year 1990 if it continues at current growth rates?* The computer creates a new column which could be named "Population Projection to 1990." Successive columns could project additional years. *What* would the total world population be in 1990 *if* India and Indonesia lowered their current growth rates of 2.05 percent each year to China's current rate of about 1 percent? Each time the operator changes any figure in the growth-rate column, the program immediately recomputes the population projection for all projected years. Subtotals could be shown for each continent. A project for class study might be to plan a world program of population restraint. Students will soon see that lowering the current growth rate of nations like Saudi Arabia from its high 4.95 percent is not going to slow world growth very much.

A main strength of data processing is that it allows students to become producers of inferences and generalizations rather than constant consumers of textbook wisdom. The computer cannot solve problems. It only follows directions, but with a data-base program, it is a tireless worker. It can process information by sorting, charting, graphing, mapping, and calculating. In the past, a great many important social studies problems were impractical because they took forever if done with paper, pencil, and brains. With the aid of a computer, students can investigate social studies subjects at increasing levels of sophistication. The textbook remains vital because it is superior in narrating the basic structure of any discipline. Together, computer and textbook make a winning combination.

> *With the aid of a computer, students can investigate social studies subjects at increasing levels of sophistication.*

A Sample Project Using the *Social Studies Tool Kit*. This program offers both abundant data and processing tools. There are two programs currently available—one using U.S. data and the other providing data on nations of the world. The states program contains 284 files of political, geographic, economic, and social information on every state. Related to the earlier questions on divorce, the program will print the two files on divorce rate and income per capita. In one suggested exercise, students paste the ranked files on left and right sides of a sheet of paper and draw lines from the name of each state on the divorce file to the same state's name on the income file as shown in Figure 3. Is divorce related to income? There is a distinct tendency for states with high divorce rates to be low in income per capita. All the top income states have low divorce rates. Why should this be so? Several states, for example, Nevada, Alaska, and North Dakota, run against the trend. Students can suggest hypotheses that may often be tested using other files of information.

This program will correlate any two files. The computer does all the calculation automatically. In this case the correlation is a surprisingly modest $R = -.24$. Correlation is one of the best approaches to studying cause and effect. Any files that have a high positive or negative correlation can be

Social Problem Solving Using a Data Base

Figure 3. Relating Divorce Rate to Per Capita Income

```
DIVORCES AND ANNUL/M POP '86                    INCOME $/C '87

RANK    STATE           DATA            RANK    STATE           DATA
----------------------------------      ----------------------------------
 1  NEVADA              14.00            1  CONNECTICUT         20980
 2  OKLAHOMA             7.50            2  NEW JERSEY          20067
 3  ALASKA               7.20            3  MASSACHUSETTS       18926
 4  ARIZONA              7.10            4  NEW YORK            18055
 5  WYOMING              7.00            5  ALASKA              17866
 6  ARKANSAS             7.00            6  MARYLAND            17722
 7  FLORIDA              6.60            7  CALIFORNIA          17661
 8  ALABAMA              6.20            8  NEW HAMPSHIRE       17133
 9  TENNESSEE            6.10            9  ILLINOIS            16347
10  NEW MEXICO           6.00           10  VIRGINIA            16322
11  TEXAS                6.00           11  DELAWARE            16238
12  IDAHO                6.00           12  NEVADA              15958
13  COLORADO             5.90           13  COLORADO            15862
14  WASHINGTON           5.80           14  MINNESOTA           15783
15  OREGON               5.70           15  WASHINGTON          15444
16  MISSISSIPPI          5.40           16  HAWAII              15366
17  MONTANA              5.30           17  RHODE ISLAND        15355
18  GEORGIA              5.30           18  MICHIGAN            15330
19  KENTUCKY             5.20           19  FLORIDA             15241
20  MISSOURI             5.10           20  PENNSYLVANIA        14997
21  WEST VIRGINIA        5.10           21  KANSAS              14952
22  KANSAS               5.10           22  WISCONSIN           14659
23  UTAH                 5.10           23  OHIO                14543
24  OHIO                 5.00           24  MISSOURI            14537
25  NORTH CAROLINA       5.00           25  NEBRASKA            14341
26  DELAWARE             4.90           26  IOWA                14191
27  MAINE                4.70           27  GEORGIA             14098
28  CALIFORNIA           4.70           28  VERMONT             14061
29  NEW HAMPSHIRE        4.60           29  ARIZONA             14030
30  VERMONT              4.40           30  OREGON              13887
31  VIRGINIA             4.30           31  INDIANA             13834
32  HAWAII               4.30           32  TEXAS               13764
33  MICHIGAN             4.10           33  MAINE               13720
34  ILLINOIS             4.00           34  NORTH CAROLINA      13155
35  SOUTH CAROLINA       4.00           35  NORTH DAKOTA        13061
36  NEBRASKA             3.90           36  WYOMING             12759
37  RHODE ISLAND         3.80           37  TENNESSEE           12738
38  NEW JERSEY           3.70           38  OKLAHOMA            12520
39  SOUTH DAKOTA         3.70           39  SOUTH DAKOTA        12511
40  IOWA                 3.60           40  MONTANA             12255
41  MARYLAND             3.50           41  KENTUCKY            11950
42  WISCONSIN            3.50           42  SOUTH CAROLINA      11858
43  PENNSYLVANIA         3.40           43  IDAHO               11820
44  NEW YORK             3.40           44  ALABAMA             11780
45  MASSACHUSETTS        3.40           45  NEW MEXICO          11673
46  NORTH DAKOTA         3.30           46  LOUISIANA           11362
47  MINNESOTA            3.30           47  ARKANSAS            11343
48  CONNECTICUT          2.90           48  UTAH                11246
49  INDIANA              NO DATA        49  WEST VIRGINIA       10959
50  LOUISIANA            NO DATA        50  MISSISSIPPI         10204
```

related in a half dozen possible ways. The program helps students treat correlation realistically and see through the many flimsy assignments of cause and effect that appear in the media and in everyday conversation.

To analyze the relationship between divorce rate and education, *The Social Studies Tool Kit* displays a bar graph of the percentage of population with at least a high school diploma in each state and points to states that are highest in divorce. The result is presented in Figure 4. Educational level does not appear to be related to divorce rate in any consistent manner.

The program will also map the rate of divorce (or any other file) into seven regions as shown in Figure 5. In this case, an artificially high rate in Nevada is removed from the list so that the distinctions among other states are clearer. To perform any of these operations without a computer would take hours. The *Statistical Abstract* and similar data sources have been available for years but only with the appearance of computers has it become possible to use these data effectively in instruction.

2. What classroom equipment is necessary for serious data processing?

A social studies classroom needs at least one computer, a printer, and appropriate software. For class problem solving, students must be able to see the computer screen. A "projection panel" attaches to the computer and sits on an overhead projector. Anything appearing on the computer screen shows up on the regular classroom movie screen. Some schools use several large monitors but students far from the screen are likely to have difficulty seeing clearly. For small-group problem solving, several computers are needed. Time in a computer lab is ideal for highly committed teachers, but in most cases permanently installed equipment in the regular classroom is more practical. A good data base containing an abundance of information can be used on the spur of the moment to clarify some aspect of a lesson or for examining a story on the morning news. Perhaps this is the way a well-informed citizen in the year 2000 will use a home computer.

3. How should social data processing be built into instruction?

A two-week unit on data processing in the classroom of some inspired teacher is *not* a good approach. Social studies teachers must realize that data processing is not a separate topic as much as a common approach to learning in all subjects. Locally developed curriculum plans should routinely suggest activities for using a data base to

Figure 4. High School Graduation and Divorce Rates

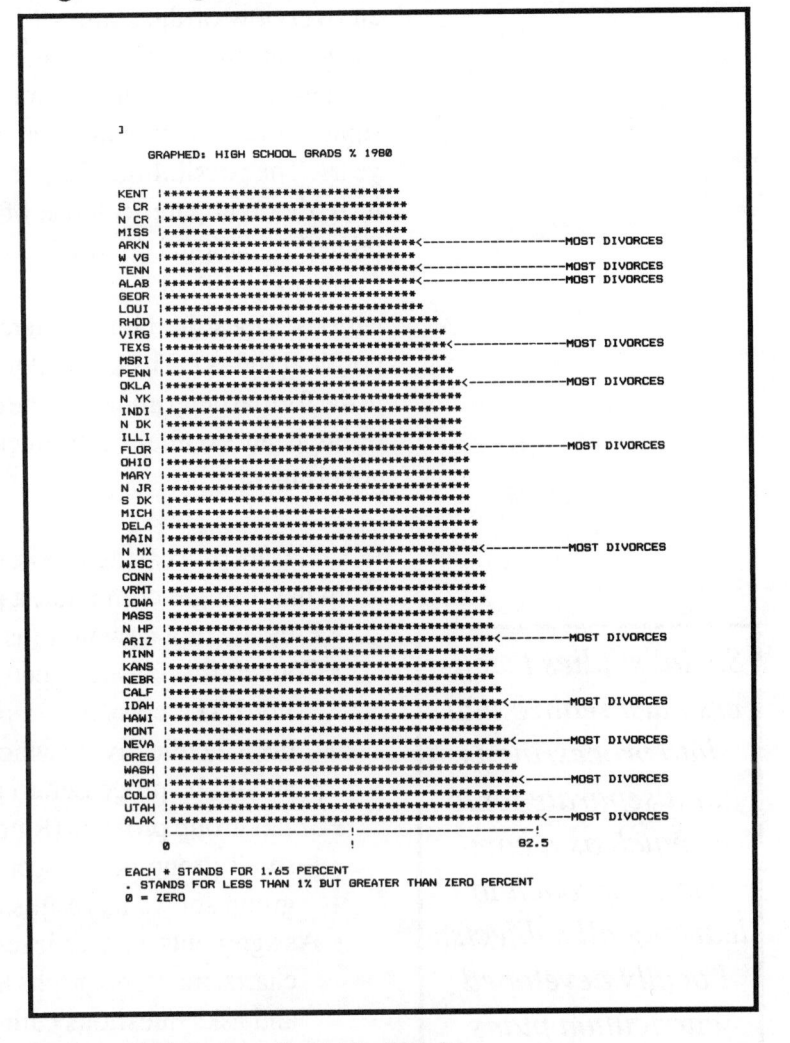

Figure 5. Divorce Rate by Region

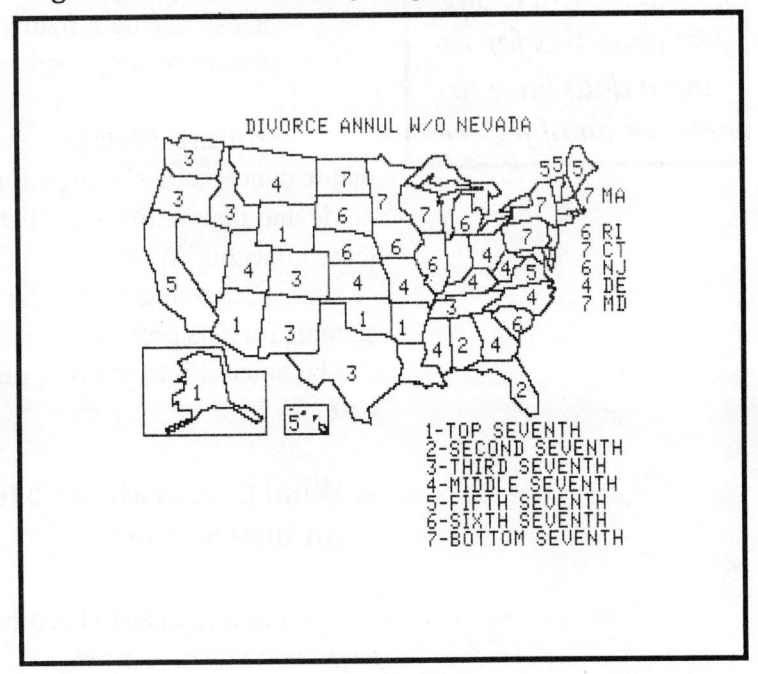

Social Problem Solving Using a Data Base

achieve an objective. For example, a course in citizenship could begin with an overview of the status of democracy in nations throughout the world. Each year, an organization named Freedom House rates the political rights in each nation on a scale from 1 to 7. With a well-stocked data base, political rights in the world can be graphed, mapped, and compared to previous years. The possibilities for good problems abound. How do political rights in Africa compare to those of South America? How are political rights related to national wealth? How are political rights related to education? Compare political rights ratings of NATO nations with the Warsaw Pact nations. Does the United States supply foreign aid to nations lacking in political rights? The computer and data base quickly provide information in the format determined by the operator. The worldwide survey of political rights is an excellent introduction (or culmination) to the study of U.S. government.

Data processing is possible in most phases of instruction if a classroom has a single computer, a printer, and a well-stocked data base.
- Preview of a new unit (as illustrated above with political rights)
- Cooperative class projects or problems (Is birth rate related to education? The class uses a projection panel and overhead projector to decide collectively which files to call to the screen and how the files should be processed to arrive at an answer.)
- Small group projects (Rate the quality of life in each U.S. state. Each small group needs access to a computer. At the conclusion, each group shows its results and explains its procedure.)
- Assignments and quizzes (The teacher prints out and duplicates charts, maps, or graphs using information related to the unit at hand and asks questions calling for interpretation.)
- Challenge projects or research papers (Is there more crime in poorer states? Create a map showing the amount of crime related to the amount of police protection.)

Social studies teachers must realize that data processing is not a separate topic as much as a common approach to learning all subjects. Locally developed curriculum plans should routinely suggest activities for using a data base to achieve an objective.

To plan for data processing in a unit of study, the teacher starts with major concepts designated for emphasis by the textbook or curriculum guide and then peruses the list of data files to find information related to these concepts. When a fit is discovered the teacher decides which form of data processing to use in instruction. Frequently new information suitable for data processing in a unit will turn up in the media. The new data can be entered into the program and related to any other files in the data base.

4. What preparation do teachers need to use data processing in instruction?

For a teacher to become comfortable with serious data processing requires about five to eight hours of initial preparation. For the totally uninitiated, some personal help is useful in getting the computer operating, inserting a disk, etc. A social studies department could schedule several training sessions on the data base software that the department selects. From then on, experience develops proficiency. Coordination with data processing in science, mathematics, and business courses makes good sense.

A decade into life with personal computers finds some teachers "converted" and about the same proportion actively "antagonistic." Most are still on the fence. Data processing has not been explored enough in social studies to know its full importance in instruction, but early signs are positive. The situation calls for our most capable and innovative teachers to lead the exploration.

Data processing is possible in most phases of instruction if a classroom has a computer, a printer, and a well-stocked data base.

References

Appleworks, Mountain View, California, 1984.

Bank Street Filer. San Rafael, California: Broderbund, 1986.

Friendly Filer. Danbury, Connecticut: Intensional Educations, 1984.

Hail to the Chief. Cherry Hill, New Jersey: CompuWare, 1984.

pfs: File, Report, Graph. Jefferson City, Missouri: Scholastic, 1985.

Social Studies Tool Kit: States and World. Green Bay, Wisconsin: Great Lakes Software and Tom Snyder Productions, 1989.

Can Numbers Be Trusted ?

Numbers are like people in that some are more trustworthy than others. In working with social information, you should always be suspicious of the accuracy of the data. Some things to be cautious about follow:

1. Watch out for numbers on topics difficult to measure or count. For example, statistics on child abuse or cases of AIDS are questionable because the people involved are likely to prefer to go unreported. Knowing that this may be true gives a different perspective on crime statistics which are so widely quoted. Watch out for opinion surveys, because they are easily misrepresented by poor sampling or by using "loaded" questions.

2. Watch out for "elastic" words. A term like 'unemployment' seems clear-cut. Either a person has a job or not. Closer scrutiny reveals all kinds of problems. Do you count as unemployed those who seek part-time work—perhaps for only a few hours per week? Do you count those who become discouraged and are no longer looking for a job?

3. Watch out for "estimates." The government has a population census once in ten years. Between times, it makes estimates on many topics. Government estimates are normally quite reliable, but mistakes are possible and bound to occur. Estimates by special-interest groups are even more suspect.

4. Watch out for files that do not reveal the source or that have a special interest group as a source. Information gatherers tend to find what they hope to find. Environmentalists are attracted to figures supporting their cause and may accept them too readily. The same is true of growth-oriented business people.

5. Watch the date on files. On some topics—such as climate or areas of states—change is usually slow so older data are likely to remain reliable. On other topics—such as unemployment or population—the changes are continual and often substantial. Old data may be questionable.

6. Watch out for data that are widely variable within the area of measurement. A file on average temperature or altitude of a state is obviously questionable. Think of a state like California that ranges far from north to south and has cold mountains as well as low desert land. It is obvious that an average temperature or altitude for a state is of questionable value. Often overlooked, however, is that variation in unemployment or crime or votes for Republicans varies within states as much as altitude and temperature.

In the social sciences, it is often necessary to use information that is less than perfect. Some information is so suspect that it should be discarded completely. But there is a gray area in which a difficult choice must be made on whether or not to use tarnished data. If your decision is to go ahead with it, the consumers should be alerted to the shortcomings of the information. Charts and graphs look precise and scientific. Do not let appearances overshadow the shaky quality of some information.

Chapter 9

School Media Programs in the Information Age
Daniel Callison

The opportunity for teachers and students to gather and use information from a variety of formats will depend greatly on the extent of cooperation between the teacher and the school library media specialist. During the coming decade, more than ever before, full-time professional library media specialists will be needed at all levels of education, elementary through secondary, to guide library users in methods for acquiring materials and gaining understanding of how to use information effectively. On-line database systems, CD-ROM formatted data bases, and video information transmitted from tape, disk, or satellite are already becoming common elements of the school library media center collection. More important for consideration here, however, is the change that must take place in the roles established by the teacher and the library media specialist to support the learning environment in the Information Age.

> *The social studies teacher and the school library media specialist must work as a team and share responsibilities for lesson planning, lesson presentation, and student evaluation.*

National Guidelines

In 1988, the American Association of School Librarians and the Association for Educational Communications and Technology issued new national guidelines for school library media programs (AASL and AECT 1988). The mission of the library media program is to ensure that students and staff are effective users of ideas and information. This mission is accomplished by

- providing intellectual and physical access to materials in all formats

- providing instruction to foster competence and stimulate interest in reading, viewing, and using information ideas

- working with other educators to design learning strategies to meet the individual needs of students

The mission of the school library media program encompasses a number of specific objectives:

1. To provide intellectual access to information through systematic learning activities that develop cognitive strategies for selecting, retrieving, analyzing, evaluating, synthesizing, and creating information at all age levels and in all curriculum content areas.

2. To provide physical access to information through (a) carefully selected and systematically organized collections of diverse learning

resources, representing a wide range of subjects, levels of difficulty, communication formats, and technological delivery systems; (b) access to information and materials outside the library media center and the school building through such mechanisms as interlibrary loan, networking and other cooperative agreements, and on-line or CD-ROM searching of computer formatted data bases; and (c) providing instruction in the operation of equipment necessary to use the information in any format for both students and teachers.

3. To provide learning experiences that encourage users to become discriminating consumers and skilled creators of information through introduction of the full range of communications media and the use of new and emerging technologies.

4. To provide leadership, instruction, and consulting assistance in the use of instructional and information technology and the use of sound instructional design principles.

5. To provide resources and activities that contribute to lifelong learning, while accommodating a wide range of differences in teaching and learning styles and in instructional methods, interests, and capacities.

6. To provide a facility that functions as the information center of the school, as a locus for integrated, interdisciplinary, intergrade, and schoolwide learning activities.

7. To provide resources and learning activities that represent a diversity of experiences, opinions, social and cultural perspectives, supporting the concept that intellectual freedom and access to information are prerequisite to effective and responsible citizenship in a democracy.

Teaching Methods for the Information Age

Five specific examples of teaching methods have appeared in the library literature over the past few years. Each provides a framework for planning social studies lessons that require extensive use of information beyond the limitations of the typical textbook. Each example or model contributes to the overall concept that the social studies teacher and the school library media specialist must work as a team and share responsibilities for lesson planning, lesson presentation, and student evaluation. As the school library media specialist moves more in the direction of sharing the role of the classroom teacher, so must the teacher move to take more responsibility in traditional tasks of the school library media specialist. The new role for the teacher would include evaluation and selection of interdisciplinary materials for the library collection, teaching information search and location skills, and teaching skills

---

> √ *distinguishing between verifiable facts and value claims*
> √ *determining the reliability of a source*
> √ *determining the factual accuracy of a statement*
> √ *distinguishing relevant from irrelevant information*
> √ *detecting bias*

that allow students to present their own information products such as charts, video programs, slide-tape programs, information newspapers, or special displays of artifacts.

The Free-Inquiry Method (Bruner 1961; Callison 1986; Jay 1987; Kay and Young 1986; Sheingold 1986; Victor 1974). Learning is process-oriented and question-oriented. The basic measure of student performance is based on these activities: (a) How extensively do students grow in the process of raising their own questions for inquiry? (b) Do students interact with other students to organize the information gathered by peers to support an overall theme to convey ideas to the rest of the school population or community? (c) How well do students employ the process of searching for answers to questions through the use of a variety of resources including charts, maps, interviews, surveys, and additional materials located beyond the school? Both the teacher and the school library media specialist work to establish the information-seeking environment and must move to the role of helping students raise and evaluate questions for inquiry as opposed to allowing the teacher or the textbook to dictate all of the questions to be investigated. Teachers and librarians may be role models who serve as researchers and demonstrate how they raise and seek answers to questions of their own related to the topic explored by the class.

The Resource-Based Method (Loertscher 1988; Printz 1984; Sitton 1980; Sitton 1981; Turner 1986; Wigginton 1976). Students seek information relevant to their local community and local history. Students must receive training in effective approaches to interviewing local personalities, editing the most useful information from audio- or videotapes, selecting the most effective photographs or slides, and presenting their "oral history." The common student products include video or slide-tape programs, a photo essay along with documentation from interviews and reference books, or a newspaper or pamphlet of interesting facts concerning local tradition or customs. Often formal presentations are made of the student products to the parents and invited community guests during an evening open house held in the school. Equipment operation, scheduling production facilities, and assistance in making contacts with local personalities are all functions that are tied to the school library media center.

> √ *identifying unstated assumptions*
> √ *identifying ambiguous or equivocal claims or arguments*
> √ *recognizing logical inconsistencies or fallacies in a line of reasoning*
> √ *distinguishing between warranted or unwarranted claims*
> √ *determining the strength of an argument*

The Critical-Thinking Method (Jay 1986; Krapp 1988; Mancall, Aaron, and Walker 1986). Information search and use exercises are based on the following skills that serve as learning objectives: distinguishing between verifiable facts and value claims; determining the reliability of a source; determining the factual accuracy of a statement; distinguishing relevant from irrelevant information; detecting bias; identifying unstated assumptions; identifying ambiguous or equivocal claims or arguments; recognizing logical inconsistencies or fallacies in a line of reasoning; distinguishing between warranted or unwarranted claims; and determining the strength of an argument. If the teacher and the library media specialist are to succeed in teaching such skills, two conditions must be met: first, the student must be developmentally ready to learn the skill; and second, the student must realize that the use of the skill will be effective in solving a personal cognitive problem. Information management skills instruction must be broad and more process-oriented. Focus must go beyond locational skills and "correct answers" and move to strategies that will help students develop insight and facility in structuring successful approaches to solving their information needs. Greater information needs that result from the demand for students to practice data comparison and judgment skills will lead to increased use of resource networking among schools and with local public and college libraries.

The Mediation Method (Kuhlthau 1985b; Liesener 1985). The primary function performed by the school library media specialist can be viewed as a mediation function. From this perspective, the specialist plays the role of an intermediary between the incredibly complex and rapidly expanding information world and the client. The concept of *intermediary* implies that some assistance is frequently required for clients or users to interact effectively and efficiently with the information world. The term 'information' is used here in its broadest sense to include all representations of ideas, including the arts, and in any media format. The school library media specialist must not only be knowledgeable in helping students locate a "table of statistical information," for example, but also be able to help them interpret the table. Mediation is also a necessary function in developing the framework so students can seek and use information beyond the school, motivating students' interest, and rewarding the students' efforts. Time planning and initial information search experience exercises, independent of the routine mechanics of completing the term paper, allow students to understand the information search process. The process itself may become more valued by the student than the end product or term paper.

The Whole-Language Method (Graves 1983; Hansen 1987; Hartse, Short, and Burke 1988; Kulleseid 1985). Writing is viewed as a process that allows one to communicate and document. In terms of social studies, writing is the essential process for recording history. Students learn to value writing and communicate effectively with writing when they are placed in the position of authors who must communicate with one another. Students become critical judges of writing when they take the roles of editor, reviewer, and even publisher. The teacher and the library media specialist facilitate the experience by keeping the classroom and the library well stocked with resource materials.

The New Information Technologies

Since the mid-1980s, many public school library media specialists have started to consider seriously access to data-base systems. Three events have supported this consideration. First, each year since 1980, the number of microcomputer units per school has increased. Many units are now available for the purpose of accessing on-line data bases.

Second, although on-line charges remain rather high for most public school budgets, more and more on-line information systems have started to offer special price structures for the public school population. Many specialized data bases may run several hundred dollars per hour of search time. Information systems that contain popular magazines, newspapers, and other reports useful to the typical secondary school student have been priced at less than $50 per on-line hour. Coupled with this marketing approach to attract the school-level buyer is the commitment on the part of school administrators to reinvest in the school library media program. Budgets, very healthy in the 1960s, are once again increasing for the specific purpose of supporting information technology (Tenopir 1986).

> *On-line information systems have started to offer special price structures for the public school population.*

Third, and most dramatic of all, is the growth in the number of information resources on CD-ROM. The disk format allows students or teachers to search for an extensive time without on-line charges. Initial investment of a few hundred dollars will allow the data base to be available in the schools not only for the experienced user but for training the novice searcher as well. The variety of CD-ROM information banks is likely to increase greatly during the coming decade. Today, several major vendors such as H.W. Wilson, NewsBank, and Information Access offer the public school market affordable disk systems with student access to hundreds of popular magazines, newspapers, and reports. In addition, some vendors are also marketing complete microfilm collections of newspapers, periodicals, or magazine articles so that students will have immediate access to a full-text copy of the information once they have located a relevant citation through the data-base search.

The future looks very exciting for CD-ROM formatted information tools. In addition to the data bases, the expanded microfiche full-text collections, and disk full-text collections, the future school library media center, elementary through secondary, will house computerized atlases, full-text encyclopedias, full-text almanacs, and biographical resources that contain not only printed information, but also video and audio information. What are the possibilities? From one CD-ROM station, the student can compare statistics from hundreds of tables to show longevity trends or comparisons from one country to another. The student, working at the one computer terminal, will be able to move from a map of a given country to its capital, to a street map of that city, and then shift to maps that represent the historical development of that country relevant to world history during the past centuries. Information on John Kennedy will include samples of his speeches, footage of the president delivering his message as captured by the news media. Biographical sketches of famous composers will include samples of their music. Foreign language dictionaries on CD-ROM will contain dozens of languages and give audio pronunciation. These future developments combined with the current vast array of microcomputer educational software will provide the basis for dramatic changes in the social studies curriculum (Troutner 1983).

> *The optical videodisc is now an inexpensive base format.*

A resurgence is beginning in the once faltering videodisc market (Callison 1984). Major news publishers and networks will be offering a summary of world events to schools on a videodisc format similar to the current CD-ROM format. Videodisc recordings of major events will be gathered in local school libraries and eventually keyed to the curriculum. Three events have allowed educators to begin to think in terms of such visual libraries. First, the optical videodisc is now an inexpensive base format. The old magnetic format was expensive, easy to erase, and did not have a high information storage capability. The optical disk is stable in that the signals are imprinted, and an index system allows the user to cue precisely to the visual series or a single frame wanted.

Second, optical disks have enough information storage space that indexing of single frames is possible. A key to use of massive amounts of information on a single disk is the ease with which users can search and move from one information point to another.

Third, although it is premature to make a definite statement on the issue, fair-use copyright contracts between producers and public schools should allow for more extensive use of library visual materials as teachers and students are allowed to transfer information from disk to tape and create their own instructional change of visual events (Callison 1981). Such in-house editing capabilities will allow more control by social studies teachers and allow individual instructors to give emphasis to current affairs or historical events. Further, students can engage in the process of producing their own visual record for enhancing class presentations. Overhead and large-screen projection units will allow for group viewing of such presentations.

School library media centers are moving in greater numbers each year to automated catalogs and networking (Aversa and Mancall 1987; Eisenberg 1988). In a few states (Epler 1988), school districts can now be networked with all other public and college libraries within the state system. Some public school systems have been longtime members of national networks that allow them to borrow materials from any library in the country. The trend is toward more and more school systems' joining such networks. The technology is available. The barriers seem to be lack of funding and an overabundance of "technophobia" by many educators (Aversa and Mancall 1987; Hannigan 1988). The major curricular question, however, continues to be, When teachers and students have all this information available, can they make intelligent information selections and use decisions?

Research on Secondary School Student On-line Information Use

Several major research projects have been conducted to determine whether secondary school students can effectively search on-line information data bases and whether they will use the materials identified through such searching (Callison 1989; Callison 1988; Callison and Daniels1988; Craver 1985; Dowling 1984; Edyburn 1988; Mancall and Deskins 1984; Pruitt and Dowling 1985; Walker 1983; Wozny 1982). Findings for these studies, many of them conducted with students in secondary school social studies classes, indicate that

- The experience of on-line searching generated an enthusiasm among students for the research process.

- On-line searching played a key role in the teachers' and librarians' objective to make students aware of the diversity of institutions that supply information as the process allowed them to identify new sources and recommend information centers beyond students' own school library.

- Time frames for the research assignment were lengthened so students had time to acquire materials from interlibrary loan.

- The "fill rate" for interlibrary loan services to high schools, within two weeks after the initial request, was around 75 percent, or three of four items requested were received from another library.

- Student requests for materials from other libraries did not tend to be "trivial" and students seemed highly selective in the items they requested.

- Although a low percentage of materials received through interlibrary loan were actually cited in students' papers, usually less than 30 percent of the items received, many of the items received from other libraries were so essential that students could not have completed the research assignment on their original topics without the outside material.

The major curricular question, however, continues to be, When teachers and students have all this information available, can they make intelligent information selections and use decisions?

- The higher percentage of filled requests tended to be for magazine or periodical articles, and the lower fill rate tended to be for book titles. Students, however, in all studies, consistently used a higher percentage of the books acquired than periodical articles acquired.

- In general, access to computer-driven data bases seemed to encourage students to seek a variety of resources and student demands, which in turn, should lead to more money for updating and enlarging school library collections left stagnant since the high investment years of the 1960s.

- The on-line and CD-ROM formatted data bases were used more extensively by students who had current affairs or contemporary issues information search topics than students who had selected historical topics. Information data bases for the secondary schools tend to cover only recent events, and students who seek in-depth information on historical events prior to 1970 will need to rely heavily on traditional printed reference materials.

- In the case of newspaper article information, students tended to locate longer or more relevant articles through the use of CD-ROM formatted index compared to use of the traditional printed index. These longer articles resulted in citation of more facts and thus a greater number of footnotes per article in the papers completed by students who had access to the CD-ROM system.

- Students tend to be more successful in searching computerized data bases through a menu selection format than through the use of a command specific search format.

- When given the opportunity, students observed searches conducted by fellow students to learn new search methods. Students should be encouraged to work together as the computer monitor provides group viewing of the search and allows students to learn from peer failure and success.

Finally, it should be noted that students, on average, learned quickly the basic search techniques, although it should be remembered that they were taught essentially simple commands or were led through the search process by menu-driven search assistance programmed specifically for an individual data base. Although such experiences introduced students to the technology and gave the students some "taste" of the Information Age, one should never dismiss the need for the experienced professional assistance from teachers and school library media specialists. With higher-level and more specialized data bases, the subject expertise of the professional information specialist is necessary to conduct a successful search.

In the public school setting, students may be able to learn quickly how to search menu-driven, popular resource data bases, and may be able to take as much time as necessary to identify leads to potentially useful materials. Professional expertise will be needed to guide students in making final decisions as to which materials to request, and how best to utilize materials effectively when they are acquired. As access to more and more information increases, the cooperative role between teachers, library media specialists, and among school libraries and other community libraries becomes essential.

Bibliography

American Association of School Librarians and Association for Educational Communications and Technology. *Information Power*. Chicago: American Library Association, 1988.

Aversa, E.S., and J.C. Mancall. "On-line Users in Schools: A Status Report." *Online* 11, no. 3 (1987): 15–36.

Aversa, E.S., and J.C. Mancall. "Managing Online Information Services in School Library Media Programs." In *School Library Media Annual*, ed. S.L. Aaron and P.R. Scales. Littleton, Colorado: Libraries Unlimited, 1986, 219–36.

Bruner, J.S. "The Act of Discovery." *Harvard Educational Review* 31 no. 1 (1961): 21–32.

Callison, D. "Fair Payment for Fair Use in Future Information Technology Systems." *Educational Technology* 21, no. 1 (1981): 20–25.

Callison, D. "Video Collections: An Uncertain but Exciting Future." *Illinois Libraries* 66, no. 7 (1984): 354–58.

Callison, D. "School Library Media Programs and Free Inquiry Learning." *School Library Journal* 32, no. 6 (1986): 20–24.

Callison, D. "Methods for Measuring Student Use of Data Bases and Interlibrary Loan Materials." *School Library Media Quarterly* 16, no. 2 (Winter 1988): 138–42.

Callison, D., and A. Daniels. "Introducing End-User Software for Enhancing Student On-line Searching." *School Library Media Quarterly* 16, no. 3 (1988): 173–81.

Callison, D. "The Secondary School Library Media Center Setting." In *On-line Searching: The Basics, Settings, and Management*, ed. J.H. Lee. Englewood, Colorado: Libraries Unlimited, 1989.

Craver, K. "Teaching On-line Bibliographic Searching to High School Students." *Top of the News* 41, no. 2 (1985): 131–38.

Dowling, K. "On-line Searching and the School Media Program." In *School Library Media Annual*, ed. S.L. Aaron and P.R. Scales. Littleton, Colorado: Libraries Unlimited, 1984, 425–35.

Edyburn, D.L. "Examining the Successful Retrieval of Information by Students Using On-line Data Bases." *School Library Media Quarterly* 16, no. 4 (1988): 256–59.

Eisenberg, M.B. "Update about Automation." In *School Library Media Annual*, ed. J.B. Smith. Englewood, Colorado: Libraries Unlimited, 1988, 130–59.

Epler, D. "Networking in Pennsylvania: Technology and the School Library Media Center." *Library Trends* 37, no. 1 (1988): 43–55.

Graves, D. *Writing: Teachers and Children at Work*. Portsmouth, New Hampshire: Heinemann, 1983.

Hannigan, J.A. "No Time for Technophobia." *School Library Journal* 35, no. 3 (1988): 29–51.

Hansen, J. *When Writers Read*. Portsmouth, New Hampshire: Heinemann, 1987.

Hartse, J.C., K.G. Short, and C. Burke. *Creating Classrooms for Authors: The Reading Writing Connection*. Portsmouth, New Hampshire: Heinemann, 1988.

Jay, M.E. "The Elementary School Library Media Teacher's Role in Educating Students to Think." *School Library Media Quarterly* 15, no. 1 (1986): 28–32.

Jay, M.E. "Designing the Library Media Program to Teach Inquiry Skills." In *School Library Media Annual*, ed. S.L. Aaron and P.R. Scales. Littleton, Colorado: Libraries Unlimited, 1987, 188–95.

Kay, L., and J.L. Young. "Socratic Teaching in Social Studies." *The Social Studies* 77, no. 4 (1986): 158–61.

Krapp, J.V. "Teaching Research Skills: A Critical-Thinking Approach." *School Library Journal* 34, no. 5 (1988): 32-35.

Kuhlthau, C.C. "A Process Approach to Library Skills Instruction." *School Library Media Quarterly* 13, no. 1 (1985a): 35-40.

Kuhlthau, C.C. *Teaching the Library Research Process: A Step-by-Step Program for Secondary School Students*. West Nyack, New York: Center for Applied Research in Education, 1985b.

Kulleseid, E.R. "Whole Language and Library Media Programs." In *School Library Media Annual*, ed. J.B. Smith. Englewood, Colorado: Libraries Unlimited (1985), 3–59.

Liesener, J.W. "Learning at Risk: School Library Media Programs in an Information World." *School Library Media Quarterly* 14, no. 1 (1985): 11–20.

Loertscher, D.V. *Taxonomies of the School Library Media Program*. Englewood, Colorado: Libraries Unlimited, 1988.

Mancall, J.C., S.L. Aaron, and S.A. Walker. "Educating Students to Think: The Role of the School Library Media Program." *School Library Media Quarterly* 15, no. 1 (1986):18–28.

Mancall, J.C., and D. Deskins. "High School Students, Libraries, and the Search Process." ERIC Document Service, ED 262 823, 1984.

Printz, M. "Topeka West's Students Honor E.T. Mom." *School Library Journal* 30, no. 8 (1984): 33–34.

Pruitt, E., and K. Dowling. "Searching for Current Information On-line." *Online* 9, no. 2 (1985): 47–50.

Sheingold, K. "Keeping Children's Knowledge Alive through Inquiry." *School Library Media Quarterly* 15, no. 2 (1986): 80–85.

Sitton, T. "Bridging the School-Community Gap: The Lessons of Foxfire." *Educational Leadership* 38, no. 3 (1980): 248–50.

Sitton, T. "Oral Life History: From Tape Recorder to Typewriter." *The Social Studies* (May-June 1981):120–25.

Tenopir, C. "On-line Data Bases: On-line Searching in the Schools." *Library Journal* 111, no. 2 (1986): 60–61.

Troutner, J. *The Media Specialist, the Microcomputer, and the Curriculum.* Littleton, Colorado: Libraries Unlimited, 1983.

Turner, P. *The School Library Media Specialist's Role: Helping Teachers Teach.* Littleton, Colorado: Libraries Unlimited, 1986.

Turner, P. *Case Studies for Helping Teachers Teach.* Englewood, Colorado: Libraries Unlimited, 1988.

Victor, E. "The Inquiry Approach to Teaching and Learning: A Primer for Teachers." *Science and Children* 12, no. 2 (1974): 23–26.

Walker, H.T. "Networking and School Library Media Centers: A Report of a Pilot Project of the Howard County Public School System and the Maryland Interlibrary Organization." *School Library Media Quarterly* 12, no. 1 (1983): 20–23.

Wigginton, E. *I Wish I Could Give My Son a Wild Raccoon.* New York: Anchor Books, 1976.

Wozny, L.A. "On-line Bibliographic Searching and Student Use of Information: An Innovative Teaching Approach." *School Library Media Quarterly* 11, no. 1 (1982): 35–42.

Chapter 10

Locating and Using ERIC and Other Data-Collection Sources

C. Frederick Risinger

It is 6:30 on a chilly November morning in Evansville, Indiana. Outside Central High School, nearly a dozen students are lined up outside the door. No, they are not basketball players waiting for the coach to open the gym so they can shoot free throws. They are social studies students waiting for the librarian in the media center. To meet student demand, she arrives at 6:30 A.M., and the media center stays open until nearly 6:00 P.M. The students are doing research in World Studies and are eager to use the data bases and other resources on the Compact Disk—Read Only Memory (CD-ROM) device attached to the computer in the media center.

Seven teachers in Montana are working on a committee that is developing districtwide plans for integrating the teaching of history and reading in the elementary grades. The time line set for them by the administration is very tight. One teacher volunteers to go to a local university library and conduct a search of the Educational Research Information Center (ERIC) data base on that topic. The next day, he has a list of 18 journal articles and 23 other documents that would appear to be helpful. Although the journal articles are readily available, the other documents are available only in microfiche form at the university. Since the teachers represent different schools, it will be difficult for all committee members to see all the reports. By making one toll-free call to the ERIC Documentation Reproduction Service (EDRS), all 23 documents are in Montana within 18 hours. Copies are made and distributed, and the committee is able to develop its recommendations in time for presentation to the school board.

When students in Leon McPherson's United States government class in Zion-Benton High School in northern Illinois are assigned research papers on contemporary social issues, they begin to set up appointments with Maggie Schmude, the school librarian. A student doing a paper on the role of the federal Department of Education in educational reform discusses her topic with Schmude and they work out a strategy for obtaining information from the ERIC system. Within a few minutes, they go on-line with the DIALOG system and obtain a printout of 30 citations including abstracts of articles, research reports, and position papers that are immediately relevant to the student's needs.

The largest and most widely used educational data base in the world is the ERIC system—and it celebrated its 20th anniversary in 1988.

Computers, Data Bases, and the Social Studies

These examples of social studies teachers using data bases for classroom instruction and curriculum development are being replicated throughout the nation. That is the good news. The bad news is that only a tiny percentage of teachers are even beginning to use the tremendous potential of ERIC and the hundreds of other data bases that are available. The vast majority of social studies teachers do not even use computers in any way. In a recent review of the literature, Ehman and Glenn (1987) reported on one national study that suggests that only 1 percent of the total use of computers in grades kindergarten through three was in social studies; 4 percent in grades four through eight; and, surprisingly, only 1 percent in grades nine through twelve. On a somewhat more positive note, Schug (1988) found that 18 percent of secondary teachers in a midwest urban district said that they had used computers to teach social studies. However, nearly half of that group had participated in the Junior Achievement Applied Economics Program that included a computer simulation.

> *The major reason social studies teachers neglect computers as a teaching tool is lack of knowledge.*

There are many good reasons for this low level of use of computers and data bases by social studies teachers. Although the number of computers in schools has quadrupled in recent years, most are in media centers or computer "labs" where science, mathematics, and computer-awareness courses occupy much of the available time. However, the major reason social studies teachers neglect computers as a teaching tool is lack of knowledge. Both Schug (1988) and Ehman and Glenn (1987) list teacher training as a major impediment.

ERIC—The Database for Educators

Surprisingly, the existence and use of computer-accessed data bases have not suddenly appeared on the educational scene. The largest and most widely used educational data base in the world is the ERIC system—and it celebrated its 20th anniversary in 1988. In DIALOG, one of the largest collections of on-line data bases, ERIC is still identified by the number "1." Based on search statistics from such services as DIALOG and Bibliographic Reference Service (BRS), the number of ERIC users is well over a million each year. That does not take into account the great number of individuals who do "hand searches" of the ERIC system using *Resources in Education* (RIE) or *Current Index to Journals in Education* (CIJE). And with the advent of CD-ROM technology, the use of ERIC is increasing dramatically. At Indiana University, librarians have had to place time restrictions on students searching the ERIC data base and estimate that usage has increased fivefold since CD-ROM equipment was added. Costs associated with CD-ROM and related data base software are declining and it is reasonable to anticipate that school systems and even individual school buildings will be able to provide access to ERIC and other data bases for both teachers and students in the near future. Although training for teachers about ERIC and how to use the system has been around for two decades, the increased access to ERIC and other data bases makes it imperative that we continue these efforts.

ERIC is an acronym for the Educational Resources Information Center. Funded by the Office of Educational Research and Improvement within the U.S. Department of Education, ERIC consists of 16 separate clearinghouses that acquire, process, and disseminate information in specialized areas of education. The ERIC Clearinghouse for Social Studies/Social Science Education (ERIC/ChESS) is assigned a "scope" that covers all aspects of history and the social sciences as they relate to education. Additionally, such topics as international education, many topics within the humanities, art and music education, and issues of gender equity are included within the scope of ERIC/ChESS. The remaining clearinghouses cover other content area scopes (such as the Clearinghouse for Science, Mathematics, and Environmental Education and the Clearinghouse for Reading and Communication Skills) or they are assigned scopes related to educational function (such as the Clearinghouse for Junior College Education or the Clearinghouse for Educational Management). At times, there are overlapping scope responsibilities. For example, if this publication were entitled "Data Generation and Interpretation in Education," the Clearinghouse on Information Resources could argue that it falls within its scope. A position paper on teaching about the greenhouse effect could be included in the scope of ERIC/ChESS or the Clearinghouse on Science, Mathematics, and Environmental Education. If the document focused on the chemical and other scientific knowledge about the greenhouse effect, the science clearinghouse would process it. On the other hand, if the paper discussed the social effects or public policy issues associated with the phenomenon, ERIC/ChESS would handle it. To the ERIC user, it makes little difference. All documents and articles that are selected and processed become part of the complete ERIC data base.

While the number of computers in schools has quadrupled in recent years, most are in media centers or computer "labs" where science, mathematics, and computer-awareness courses occupy much of the available time.

In addition to the 16 specialized clearinghouses, there are three other components to the ERIC system. Like the others, they are working under contract for the U.S. Department of Education. The ERIC Facility receives the input from all 16 clearinghouses and prepares the information for RIE, published and distributed by the Government Printing Office. The Educational Document Reproduction Service is a private company that provides the microfiche and paper copy of all the documents in the ERIC system. And Oryx Press, a private publishing house in Phoenix, prints and distributes CIJE, the compendium of information published in professional journals and other periodical literature.

When ERIC first began, it did not cover journals and periodicals. That was left to other bibliographic services like *Education Index*. Within a few years, however, the need to include articles on educational topics became clear and CIJE was initiated. It is important to point out that not all articles in every professional journal listed in CIJE are reviewed and abstracted. Only articles that deal with education are included. For example, the *Journal of the American Political Science Association* may have an excellent article on "Changing Voting Patterns in Southern States since 1964." Although the article might be an excellent source of information for a social studies teacher or student of U.S. government, it would not be selected and abstracted for the ERIC system. It is not an educational article. If the title were "Teaching about Changing Voter Behavior in Introductory College Courses," the article would be included. This discussion highlights a common misperception about ERIC—it does not include every article from all magazines in its data base. Journals are categorized as "comprehensive," "selective," and "one-shot." A comprehensive journal means that every article in each issue is covered. *Social Education, The Social Studies*, and *Teaching Political Science* are in this category. In a selective journal, only those articles that deal with education are entered into the data base. Journals from the American Historical Association or the American Sociological Association are selective. Sometimes, only one or two articles may be abstracted from an issue. A "one-shot" journal is a magazine that is not on our regularly reviewed list, but which has an article that has a definite relationship to social studies education. For example, the November 1988 issue of *The Atlantic Monthly* had a major article by Paul Gagnon entitled "Why Teach History?" That single article was abstracted and added to the ERIC database.

When educators or other ERIC users conduct a search, they will develop a list of magazine articles and documents such as research studies, conference presentations, curriculum guides, and position papers. This list will include typical bibliographic information—author(s), title, date, source, number of pages, and similar information. Additionally, there will be an abstract of the item. The abstracts of magazine articles (called "annotations" in ERIC jargon) are limited to 50 words, whereas the document abstracts may be as long as 250 words. The journal articles are not available from ERIC but can be obtained from libraries or from services such as University Microfilms, Incorporated (UMI) in Ann Arbor, Michigan. The documents are available from EDRS in Arlington, Virginia. In most cases, they are available in both microfiche or paper copy format. Microfiche are extremely inexpensive, easy to carry around, and can be read through special readers. Some microfiche readers have printing capabilities and others are small, portable devices. Many ERIC users prefer a paper copy of the document and EDRS is happy to comply. In recent years, major efforts have been made to make ERIC more "user-friendly" and to provide speedier, more efficient service. EDRS has a toll-free number (800-227-3742) and accepts both Visa and MasterCard orders. For individuals who need the documents right away, EDRS will FAX them to customers within a few hours. That is how the committee in Montana described at the beginning of this chapter received its documents overnight. Finally, for educators with telecommunications equipment, documents or microfiche can be ordered directly on-line 24 hours a day. These expanded services have dramatically increased the use of ERIC by educators and others interested in educational issues.

There is still another aspect of ERIC services for educators—one that is not directly related to the data base and yet is probably the most useful for classroom teachers. In addition to building the data base, each ERIC clearinghouse develops and disseminates its own publications. In most cases, these publications are "synthesis documents"—they extract the information from the data base and present it in a format and style that can be directly helpful to teachers, department heads, and administrators. One of the books cited earlier in this chapter is an example. *Computer-Based Education in the Social Studies* by Lee Ehman and Allen Glenn is an ERIC/ChESS publication almost entirely built on documents and articles from the ERIC database. In addition to book-length publications, each ERIC clearinghouse also publishes 10–12 "Digests" each year. A digest is a two-page typeset document that summarizes a specific topic of interest to the profession. Recent digests from ERIC/ChESS include "Critical Thinking in the Social Studies," "Teaching about Religion in the Social Studies," "The Nature of Geographic Literacy," and "Teaching about the Pacific Rim." ERIC digests are extremely useful to individual teachers and committees working on curriculum development or reviewing current trends in social studies. They contain bibliographic references to guide further research. The ERIC Digest program has become so popular nationally that the BRS data base now includes a file en-titled "ERIC Digests on Line." Digests from all 16 ERIC clearinghouses are available in full-text format. These are extremely useful for educators who are interested in the full range of topics in the ERIC system. For example, readers of this publication interested in data base use in schools will undoubtedly find interesting several digests developed by the Clearinghouse for Information Resources. Finally, ERIC/ChESS also disseminates Resource Packets as part of its publications program. Each resource packet is an expanded annotated bibliography on a specific topic in the social studies. A resource packet includes the abstracts of articles and documents in the ERIC system, names and addresses of organizations and individuals related to the topic, reviews of exemplary textbooks, audiovisual materials, and computer software, and other suggested resources. Recently published resource packets include "Teaching about Western Europe" and "Resources in Geography."

ERIC digests are extremely useful to individual teachers and committees working on curriculum development or reviewing current trends in social studies.

How Social Studies Teachers Can Use the ERIC Data Base

In its 20-year history, the ERIC system has had a perennial dilemma. Although it can lay claim to being the "largest and most widely used educational data base," it is not widely used by classroom teachers. Many, perhaps most, teachers are aware of ERIC, but they do not know what it really is or how it can help them in their everyday tasks of instruction, curriculum planning, or classroom management. To most classroom teachers, ERIC is that set of volumes on the college library reference desk where they spent hours doing

> *Today, ERIC is making a major effort to bring into the data base two types of documents previously neglected.*
>
> *The first type of document is local and state curriculum guides.*
>
> *The second type of document that is being added to ERIC in increasing numbers is teacher-developed instructional units and activities.*

research on their graduate theses. That it could be helpful to them now seems unlikely. Unfortunately, the time and equipment constraints of the typical social studies classroom teacher in the recent past supported that feeling. But this is a new time—new not just because of technological developments, but also because of very different policies in ERIC. For years, the primary audience for ERIC consisted of college-level researchers and teacher trainers. Lip service was given to serving "practitioners" (more ERIC jargon for "teachers"), but it was recognized that most classroom teachers had neither the time nor the resources to go on-line and search the ERIC data base. Moreover, what was a teacher to do with the abstracts or even the full-text documents themselves? The majority of the materials included in the data base were research studies and position papers that, although possibly relevant to their interests, were usually more detailed and complex than needed. This is a primary reason for the success of the ERIC publications program with classroom teachers. The books, digests, and resource packets synthesized the research and scholarly papers so that teachers could use the information.

But times and policies change. Not only do teachers have increased and less costly access to the ERIC data base, but the data base itself is changing. Today, ERIC is making a major effort to bring into the data base two types of documents previously neglected—both of them directly relevant and immediately useful to teacher needs. The first type of document is local and state curriculum guides. These guides range from the controversial *History–Social Science Framework for California Schools* to the thick North Carolina state curriculum packed with implementation activities for each stated objective and a local curriculum guide describing Evansville, Indiana's growth as a river city. For the first time, local curriculum development or revision committees can obtain a wide variety of models to examine and learn from. There is simply no reason for a group of busy teachers to start a curriculum review and revision project from the very beginning. There are some outstanding curriculum guides from the province of Alberta, Canada, in the ERIC data base. Moreover, there are accompanying provincewide tests for every grade level in the social studies curriculum. Teachers and supervisors around the nation are calling for materials to help them cope with questions of content, accountability, and testing. Possible answers are in the ERIC data base.

The second type of document that is being added to ERIC in increasing numbers is teacher-developed instructional units and activities. Many of these come from local and regional social studies conferences where teachers demonstrate a new instructional approach to a particular topic. Teachers enjoy seeing how their colleagues approach an issue, and although, they are unlikely to adopt the lesson or unit completely, they will adapt and borrow ideas, activities, and sources. By submitting their own or their school's units, instructional activities, and curriculum guides, these teachers gain increased recognition for themselves, their school system and, moreover, help their colleagues in the next town and throughout the nation.

Formerly, when teachers searched the ERIC data base on a topic, they received a great deal of information. Much of it would be useful and interesting, but not directly relevant to their current needs. Today, however, an ERIC search on middle school geography will retrieve not only research studies into what students know (or do not know); it will include the Five Themes of Geography from the National Council for Geographic Education and the Association of American Geographers. What is more important, teachers will find several exemplary teacher-produced classroom activities that have immediate utility.

Teachers are increasing their use of ERIC. Much of this is due to higher levels of computer literacy and the availability of equipment, both at school and at home. Howe (1986) found that teachers who had a master's degree, had attended a college or university with an ERIC collection, and were teaching in an urban or suburban area were more familiar and more likely to use ERIC than those who had not and who taught in rural areas. The most frequently praised ERIC product or service was the availability of microfiche. ERIC users appreciate the quick service they receive when they order microfiche from EDRS and the convenience of having 90 or so pages in a 4-by-6-inch space. The most common reasons for using ERIC were, in order, (1) for academic work, (2) for research on a course they were taking, (3) to identify curriculum and instructional materials, (4) to improve classroom practices, (5) to identify trends, and (6) to assist in making decisions. With the increased effort being given to adding curriculum guides and instructional materials to the data base, it is likely that the use of ERIC by classroom teachers will continue to grow.

Bibliography

Center for Advanced Technology in Education. *Extending the Human Mind: Computers in Education.* Eugene, Oregon: Center for Advanced Technology in Education, 1986.

Ehman, L.H., and A.D. Glenn. *Computer-Based Education in the Social Studies.* Bloomington, Indiana: ERIC Clearinghouse for Social Studies/Social Science Education, 1987.

Ekwurzel, D., and B. Saffran. "Low-Cost On-line Searching Techniques." *Journal of Economic Education* 18 (1987): 287–307.

Howe, R.W. *Survey of Selected ERIC Users*. Arlington, Virginia: E R I C Documentation Reproduction Service: ED 277 565, 1986.

Russ, M. *Creating and Using Databases in the Social Studies*. Indianapolis: Indiana Clearinghouse for Computer Education, 1986.

Schug, M.C. "What Do Social Studies Teachers Say about Using Computers?" *The Social Studies* 79 (1988): 112–15.

Thompson, C., and L. Vaughn. *Computers in the Classroom: Experiences Teaching with Flexible Tools*. Chelmsford, Massachusetts: Northeast Regional Exchange, Inc., 1986.

Chapter 11

How School Textbook Publishers View the Information Age

Cameron S. Moseley

This chapter takes the form of a fictitious interview between Trudy Tryall, a reporter for World Watchers, Unlimited ("an organization of concerned world citizens") and Harry Hopeyng, president of the school division of Veritas, publishing subsidiary of Pragmatics, Inc. The author believes that the views expressed and the experiences described are representative of school publishers generally. But Trudy Tryall, World Watchers, Unlimited, Harry Hopeyng, Veritas, Pragmatics, Inc., Highbridge and Lowbridge, Henry Highbridge, and Blissful, Connecticut, are his personal creations.

Trudy: How do you pronounce your last name, Mr. Hopeyng?
Harry: It rhymes with 'coping' but please call me Harry, Trudy.

Trudy: I understand you've held every job there is in school publishing.
Harry: That's more or less true. I majored in history at college and then got an M.A. in U.S. History. After teaching U.S. and world history in high school for two years, I started at Highbridge and Lowbridge as a high school textbook salesman. At various times, I've been an elementary school salesperson, field sales manager, product development manager, inventory manager, promotions manager, history editor, managing editor, editor in chief, and division head. The best secretary I ever had was annoyed because I typed as well as she did and typed many of my own letters. I still do—on a word processor. Typists take to them, you know. I've also been quite active in ATPI, AEPI, and AAP School Division affairs.

Trudy: What are the ATPI and the AEPI?
Harry: The American Textbook Publishers Institute and the American Educational Publishers Institute. The ATPI was founded in 1942. The name was changed to AEPI in the 1960s to reflect the fact that many members were publishing various instructional materials that were not basic textbooks, especially audiovisual materials. In 1970, the AEPI was merged with the American Book Publishers Council (ABPC), forming the Association of American Publishers (AAP).

Trudy: What is Highbridge and Lowbridge?
Harry: It no longer exists. It was founded in 1888 by two moonlighting college professors. When I began in 1958, our junior and senior high school U.S. history textbooks and our world history textbook were leaders in the field. We also had textbooks in world geography, civics, economics, psychology, U.S. government, and Problems of the American Democracy. And we had a few specialized literature anthologies, the high-school edition of a

The author believes that the views expressed and the experiences described in this fictitious interview are representative of school publishers generally.

college grammar/usage/rhetoric handbook, and a few moderately successful mathematics and science textbooks. Foreign language came later. Our college department was fairly strong in history and English, and we had a small but highly respected trade department. The head of the company when I signed on was Henry Highbridge, grandson of one of the founders, and a medieval history scholar as well as a publisher. He admired Harold Rugg, but he disagreed with Rugg's "social science" approach and never wanted to get into elementary school publishing. He believed the only subject that really mattered was history. "If you study history, you study everything, including geography," he would say. He used to talk about the importance of "orienting kids in time and place."

Trudy: Who was Harold Rugg?
Harry: The major author of a truly innovative social science program that began coming out in the late 1930s. The books were widely adopted, but after World War II began, just as widely dropped. Rugg was accused by some of being un-American. I remember how furious my father was when the Blissful, Connecticut, schools threw the Rugg books out. I was using one of them in the 6th grade in 1940, and I certainly didn't think they were un-American.

Trudy: Then how did you get into elementary school publishing?
Harry: Henry Highbridge controlled the company. About a year before he died he sold out to Veritas, Inc., which had successful elementary school programs in language arts, mathematics, and social studies. It was supposed to be a merger made in heaven, but, as many of us knew beforehand, the development and marketing of elementary school programs are quite different from the development and marketing of junior and senior high school textbooks. It was a nightmare for the first three years. We were called Veritas Highbridge for a while, but then Highbridge was dropped. Even though I did not come from the "surviving corporation"—what a ghastly expression!—I managed to keep my job.

Trudy: Do you have general comments about the "Information Age"?
Harry: To me, it is both discouraging and encouraging. Technology seems to be making available to us unlimited opportunities to learn more about the world and do everything better. There are times, however, when I feel that all we're really doing is accumulating and manipulating information—including a lot of misinformation—faster and faster.

School publishers became familiar with computers early on because they helped us keep track of inventory. We have a lot more inventory problems than other segments of the industry. And computers certainly have helped us to maintain more accurate and up-to-date information about the schools and to produce books and other materials faster. But I see no evidence

> *There are times, however, when I feel that all we're really doing is accumulating and manipulating information—including a lot of misinformation—faster and faster.*

whatsoever that computers have helped us make better publishing decisions. It may be possible to create accurate computer models of the future in many areas, but I have yet to see a computer model that will tell us how reading should be taught or what the elementary school social studies curriculum should look like five or ten years from now. As for market research, one of my acerbic assistants says, "We're great at raking up leaves but we don't seem to know how to get them off the lawn."

Right now at Veritas our authors and editors are trying to decide how we'll handle the 1988 presidential election in our middle school, junior high, and high school U.S. history textbooks. They'll all be out in new editions with 1990 copyrights, but they'll be coming from the bindery next summer in time for various adoption deadlines. We're up to our ears in a welter of facts and alleged facts that must be sorted out somehow. And, as you can imagine, feelings are running high. All shades of political opinion are represented in our school division, by the way!

Trudy: Are you against technology?
Harry: We couldn't function nowadays without computers, photocopiers, sophisticated phone systems, FAX machines, and the like. Word processors have proved their usefulness for authors, editors, secretaries, and just about everyone else. But on an overall basis, in terms of publishing goals, the products now being turned out don't measure up to the technology behind them. Perhaps it's because we haven't learned to use technology properly, but I don't think so.

Trudy: What's the problem, then?
Harry: It seems to me we're living in an "information-overload age." I sometimes think there's a danger the world won't end in either fire or ice but will simply drown in information. And the more information we pile up, the more misinformation we pile up along with it, and the less able we seem to be to handle it all. Furthermore, it is all too easy to say we need still more data before we can make a decision.

Shortly after we arranged this interview, the *Vincennes* shot down an Iranian airliner in the Persian Gulf. The crew of the *Vincennes* seems to have reacted incorrectly to an enormous amount of correct information. Of course, the radio that would have picked up the airliner's signals wasn't turned on, nobody had an airline schedule, and nobody used binoculars.

Trudy: How does this relate to textbooks?
Harry: Besides the presidential election, we're trying to decide what to say about the Persian Gulf generally and the *Vincennes* particularly. And there are many more data-heavy topics that are giving us headaches—AIDS, abortion, Irangate, drugs, gun control, Nicaragua, the world's religions, ethnic minorities, feminism, homosexuality, Star Wars, evolution, creation-

> *It seems to me we're living in an "information-overload age."*

ism, and so on and on. Suppose the Shroud of Turin had proved to be genuine. I call myself an agnostic Lutheran, but I think that the role of Jesus in history is perhaps the most important subject in the world. But how should this be handled in school history textbooks? Of course, by the time we decide about some of these things, I may have been fired.

Trudy: Good heavens, why?
Harry: Pragmatics is currently fighting a takeover threat and may have to sell Veritas to the highest bidder, possibly a European company. The European company will probably want to get rid of the school division, which probably will then be sold to one of the other large publishing companies with a school division. Our school list will be folded into the other company's school list and I'll be folded out. Oh well, as Kurt Vonnegut is fond of saying, "And so it goes."

Trudy: You sound a bit cynical.
Harry: Your questions and comments have reminded me that I entered publishing when educators and publishers were going into a frenzy about teaching machines and programmed instruction. Some people really seemed to think that programmed instruction would be *the* answer to all teaching and learning problems. We couldn't see it that way. Our chief history editor and I once figured out, over a couple of drinks at a sales meeting, that it would take about 500,000 frames to program a course in 12th grade U.S. history. We laughed so much the waitress came over and told us to quiet down. And I remember Henry Highbridge saying programmed instruction would never get anywhere until computers became cost-effective.

After programmed instruction, we had "the new math" and "learner validation" and "learner verification." I remember a school publishing executive at an AAP committee meeting going into orbit about the Educational Products Information Exchange (EPIE). He became violently angry because EPIE seemed to believe that they could test books more or less like toaster ovens.

We've also had "contract learning," "turnkey contracts," and the "discovery method" in social studies and science. So when you came at me with "information age," all I could think of was, "Here we go again." It seems to me that librarians and publishers—particularly educational, professional, and reference publishers—always have been dealing with huge amounts of information, even before we had all this new technology, and we always have been trying to sort it out.

By the way, you may be interested in reading Fritz Machlup's *The Production and Distribution of Knowledge in the United States* (Machlup 1962). Machlup is generally given credit for coining the term 'knowledge industry'. It's a profound and fascinating work.

> *After programmed instruction, we had "the new math" and "learner validation" and "learner verification" ... "contract learning," "turnkey contracts," "discovery method."*
>
> *So when you came at me with "Information Age," all I could think of was, "Here we go again."*

Textbook Publishers View the Information Age

Trudy: What happened to programmed instruction?
Harry: Computer software instructional programs are more or less the lineal descendants of programmed instruction. But recently I heard the head of another major school publishing house say at a seminar, "The computer software revolution is over; in fact, it never happened." I would put it another way. Nothing has yet happened to suggest that instructional computer programs as they now seem to be evolving will entirely supplant textbooks.

The same thing is true of videocassettes, which I believe are another important instructional medium. But just the other day the head of another school publishing house said to me, "We were very bullish about videocassettes a year ago, but we've found the marketing problems far worse than anticipated, and sales much lower than expected." He added, "Of course, it's still worse with computer software."

Trudy: You seem to be saying that all this new technology won't be of much use in the schools?
Harry: Oh no. What I am saying is that when you take a look at all the different kinds of instructional media including textbooks, what we used to call "printed materials of instruction," the basic textbook still appears to be the most convenient and least expensive medium available. A book, by the way, is an extraordinarily ingenious mechanical device. It requires no outside power source, except the ability to turn pages, and no other equipment besides adequate eyesight. You can browse back and forth through it without pushing buttons, and you can carry it around with you. It can be updated and revised to meet changing needs.

More than 20 years ago I heard a publisher talk about the possibility that some day a lap-top box would be developed that would contain a library of hundreds or even thousands of volumes. Any desired reference could be found quickly and easily, and page after page could be made to appear, as needed, on a screen on one side of the box. It would have a self-contained power source. Something like that could certainly replace textbooks as they now exist, but we still haven't seen that box.

By the way, some people appear to believe that all textbooks are stodgy, unimaginative, and dull, that school publishers are just like their products, and that they're opposed to the so-called new media. Nothing could be farther from the truth. We have been experimenting with all kinds of nonprint media for more than three decades, and some of us have lost quite a bit of money doing so.

Despite all the excitement about how much the kids are learning through computers, and how easily they're taking to computers, there's really not much agreement about how computers should be used in schools. A person

> *Nothing has yet happened to suggest that instructional computer programs as they now seem to be evolving will entirely supplant textbooks.*

who has his own company in this area told me a few months ago that his estimate of the entire computer software market for both schools and colleges was about $300 million in annual sales, as compared with an estimated $1.7 billion spent in 1987 on K–12 textbooks (AAP statistics). I think his estimate may be high. This same person believes that computer software programs and print materials should go hand in hand.

Trudy: You seem to think textbooks will change as a result of new technology.

Harry: I hope they will, but I'm not quite sure. A textbook, any textbook, should be a guide to a course, not the course itself. It should lead both teachers and students to the classroom library, if there is one, and beyond that to the school library—pardon me, media center. These places should be filled with books, videocassettes, computer software, etc., to add new dimensions to what the students have read and discussed in class. This conceivably could lead to a reduction in the size and price of textbooks, and meet to some extent the criticism of textbook bashers that textbooks, particularly history textbooks, are much too large. But for these developments to occur, there would have to be major changes in the way schools adopt and use instructional materials. And there would have to be budget increases for both textbooks and library materials.

> *Only about 2 percent of the operating expenses of schools go toward instructional materials.*

Trudy: Should schools spend more on instructional materials?

Harry: I was hoping you'd ask. Now I want to ask *you* a question. What percentage of the operating expenses of schools goes toward the purchase of instructional materials?

Trudy: I suppose about 5 or 6 percent.

Harry: It's about 2 percent. This means that only about $60 per student was spent in 1987 on instructional materials of *all* kinds in *all* subjects at *all* grade levels. And only about $9 of that went toward the purchase of social studies materials.

Trudy: I'm shocked.
Harry: I hoped you would be.

Trudy: Is anything being done about it?
Harry: Not very much. I heard a marketing specialist from outside the industry say, at a recent AAP School Division meeting, that the 2 percent I mentioned "is probably a given; you'll probably have to accept it, since it's always been that way." That's the wrong attitude, in my opinion, and in the opinion of most school publishers.

Trudy: But I thought textbooks were so profitable.
Harry: It's a relatively solid, stable industry, but the "vast amounts of

cash generated by best-selling textbooks," in the words of one textbook basher, are a myth. Yes, the profit margin on a *successful* textbook or program is good, but there are lots of *unsuccessful* textbooks. The profits of the entire school publishing industry, very broadly defined, were probably between $150 million and $200 million in 1987. IBM's profits were probably around $4 to $5 *billion*. And when I say the entire school publishing industry, I'm including hundreds of smaller companies as well as the very large basic textbook publishers. And please remember that you cannot develop new programs without profits.

Trudy: How much should be spent on instructional materials?
Harry: When I first became active in ATPI affairs, we talked about trying to double the present percentage. The 5 to 6 percent you guessed previously seems to me about the right amount.

Trudy: Then what would happen?
Harry: For one thing, a U.S. history textbook could be published in three or four smaller and more easily handled volumes. The price would be higher, of course. And a school would be able to buy sets of different textbooks with different points of view for the same classroom, plus supplementary classroom materials of various other kinds. Teachers should not have to depend on just one textbook. The chief benefit of higher budgets would be that teachers and students would have access to a much wider range of materials and points of view.

Trudy: I've heard that computers and desk-top publishing will make it possible for publishers to produce all kinds of variations of their textbooks to meet the specific curriculum requirements of different school districts, and for school districts to produce some of their own textbooks. What do you think?
Harry: It's theoretically possible, but impossible in practice, in my view, and also not desirable except in very specialized situations. It would increase the cost of textbooks, and it would be an administrative and logistical nightmare. My wife says I'm like the Terrible Tempered Mr. Bangs when I get started on that subject.

Trudy: Who's the Terrible Tempered Mr. Bangs?
Harry: A character in Toonerville Trolley, a wonderful comic strip that used to run in the *New York Herald Tribune*. He'd jump up and down and yell when he was angry, which was all the time. The only one who could handle him was the Powerful Katrinka. She could handle anybody—man, woman, or beast. Speaking of comic strips, I think the comic-strip technique is an overlooked and underrated instructional medium in this country. You could teach U.S. history, and very sound history too, by using comic-strip techniques. There's an idea for a new kind of publishing company, incidentally.

Trudy: You sound somewhat discouraged.
Harry: I am, at least part of the time.

Trudy: Why? You say textbooks will have their place for a long time to come, and you seem to like school publishing.
Harry: First, I'm particularly discouraged about instructional materials budgets and even more discouraged that, up to now, no serious, concerted efforts have been made to raise the national consciousness about the situation. It seems to me scandalous that the amount spent per student each year on instructional materials is less than the price of a couple of tickets to a hit show in New York City.

Second, I'm more and more concerned about the bad effects that textbook adoption procedures, and particularly state-adoption procedures, are having on the quality of textbooks and how they are produced, particularly in the elementary grades. A leading publisher who said to me a couple of years ago that "all the textbooks look alike" wasn't far wrong. Most of us feel we'd all be better off if the whole country were "open territory," with each district making its own buying decisions. I recommend for your special attention Harriet Tyson-Bernstein's *A Conspiracy of Good Intentions: America's Textbook Fiasco* (1988). In my opinion, the Council for Basic Education (CBE) is doing a lot of good work.

Third, the depositories mandated in many state-adoption states are an anachronism that costs the industry extra millions of distribution dollars and adds to the price of textbooks. The recent bankruptcy of the Texas School Book Depository, which hurt several companies badly, may make some other depository walls come tumbling down. I hope so.

Fourth, long-term state adoption price contracts, sometimes up to six years, are yet another anachronism that adds to the price of textbooks.

Fifth, I continue to be disheartened and dismayed that what school publishers have learned about the curriculum from continually talking with teachers and supervisors tends to be overlooked when commissions are appointed to study this or that educational problem.

In that connection, I was greatly heartened by the NCSS–AAP School Division conference in Arlington, Virginia, in March 1988. It was the best meeting of educators and publishers that I have ever attended. It occurs to me that one of the reasons may be that, as I see it, there are more problems and complexities in the social studies curriculum for both educators and publishers than in all the rest of the skills and subject areas combined.

Sixth, I particularly wish that textbook bashers outside the industry would take the trouble to find out more about school publishing before

> *It seems to me scandalous that the amount spent per student each year on instructional materials is less than the price of a couple of tickets to a hit show in New York City.*

sounding off so stridently about the shortcomings of school publishers and school textbooks.

Seventh, I'm concerned about the state of the social studies curriculum, and especially the K–6 social studies curriculum. We went through a fruitless exercise recently trying to determine the common threads that ran through the courses of study of states and larger cities. There didn't seem to be any. This may relate to my feeling, expressed above, that K–12 social studies is incredibly complicated. I don't think California has developed *the* answer!

Eighth, and this is my biggest worry, I am very deeply troubled about what's happening to the industry as a result of the current wave of acquisitions and mergers, and the continuing anxiety about what's going to happen to major companies. I mentioned earlier that Veritas may soon be "in play." If I get fired, I'd come out of it very well financially, but some of my younger associates would not be so fortunate. It's having a bad effect on them already, and publishing efforts are suffering. Veritas has been run by publishers who are interested in publishing good books as well as producing profits, but it seems to me the only thing the top Pragmatics people worry about is profits. This has meant that we haven't been able to take many real chances in recent years on developing innovative school publishing programs. We have devoted most of our energies to trying to win big state adoptions, even if it meant going to outside developers and putting up millions of dollars to get a program ready quickly to meet a deadline.

> *This has meant that we haven't been able to take many real chances in recent years on developing innovative school publishing programs.*

The educational development houses are filled with bright people, most of them out of school publishing, but I think the ideas for new publishing products—elementary social studies, for example—should be coming from combinations of first-rate scholars, first-rate teachers, and publishers. I do not understand why more college professors haven't shown interest and leadership. It's partly the fault of the publishers, but not entirely. It seems to me that scholars and educators in the social studies have shown more interest in this problem, and more awareness of the situation, than those in other areas. The fact that I was asked to express my views for this NCSS bulletin is an example.

Trudy: I don't think you should be compared with the Terrible Tempered Mr. Bangs, but you do get a bit worked up.
Harry: And you haven't heard my concluding blast.

Trudy: Oh, my!
Harry: You asked how school publishers view the "Information Age." So far I've seen no evidence that piling up more and more facts and manipulating them faster and faster with more and more sophisticated technology is really helping us to work "smarter." We have all kinds of new tools, and many of us are using these tools with great skill, but I don't think we're using them very intelligently. What happened on the *Vincennes*

unfortunately seems to be typical of what's happening everywhere in our society.

Trudy: Is there anything else you want to say?
Harry: Some good news and some bad news. The bad news is a *1984*-type story I heard the other day. In order to sell a history textbook in a state that will be nameless, a publisher was advised to remove the cigarette holder from a photograph of Franklin D. Roosevelt, even though this was one of FDR's "trademarks." I've never smoked in my life, but I find this ridiculous and dishonest. Unfortunately, it's typical of what school publishers are being asked to do all the time.

> *So far I've seen no evidence that piling up more and more facts and manipulating them faster and faster with more and more sophisticated technology is really helping us to work "smarter."*

The good news is that, despite my occasional fits of bad temper, I think school publishing is a great business to be in. Most of us like what we're doing, like schools and school people, have a genuine interest in education, and would like to make more contributions than we're making now. We hope that scholars, teachers, and publishers will be able to get together in new ways, and to develop innovative new programs that will take full advantage of new technology, and will lead to new kinds of school publishing ventures in new kinds of companies, not necessarily large companies.

Getting back to the importance of history, Henry Highbridge used to say, "One thing you can always count on; things will continue to happen in chronological order."

Trudy: You seem to be "hoping" as well as "coping." Good luck!

References

Machlup, Fritz. *The Production and Distribution of Knowledge in the United States.* Princeton, New Jersey: Princeton University Press, 1962.

Tyson-Bernstein, Harriet. *A Conspiracy of Good Intentions: America's Textbook Fiasco.* Washington, D.C.: Council for Basic Education, 1988.

Chapter 12

Human Dimensions of the Information Age

Margaret A. Laughlin
H. Michael Hartoonian
Norris M. Sanders

No one disputes the reality of an Information Age. From farm to factory to the family car, we encounter computers and other information processors that signal a new evolutionary course as far-reaching as that wrought by the printing press in the 15th century. A temptation in this concluding chapter is to describe a well-informed citizen in the year 2000 as studying complex social issues by marshalling and manipulating platoons of relevant data from a public information utility using the powers of a home computer. At least in part, the vision may prove true but it is too speculative to be useful in the present. As an alternative, we focus on the implications of the evidence and arguments put forth in this bulletin on schools as they exist today.

The Curriculum

The structure of knowledge that we use in our curriculum bulletins and textbooks is not in need of essential change. The main concepts and generalizations from the social science disciplines continue to deserve greater emphasis than the masses of facts. The major change is the growing volume of fine-grained data. Just as the microscope, telescope, and similar instruments expanded the amount of data available to physical scientists, so new instuments and social inventions have expanded the data available on the social world. Most curriculum bulletins and textbooks have focused attention on concepts, generalizations, and skills for several decades. Still in classroom interrogation, recitation, and testing, the emphasis has too often been on factual recall. The popular volume on cultural literacy accentuates memory. Without question, the ability to recall many political, historical, geographic, economic, and social facts is an advantage to a citizen in any age. The problem is that with limited learning time, the memorization of facts can result in neglect of the application of the more important and rapidly growing number of concepts, generalizations, and skills.

Within the broad and relatively stable curricular framework, we will need frequent adjustment.

The information explosion does not upset the validity of alternative "scope and sequence" recommendations endorsed by the National Council for the Social Studies (*Social Education*, November/December 1986). Major goals for the social studies should continue to call for preparation for intelligent, active citizenship and competence in private economic and social life. Goals should also continue to call for cognitive, affective, and aesthetic learning. The necessary educational adjustments that are apparent in these early stages of the Information Age have to do with using more data and more concepts and developing a new group of skills. Information technology is responsible for most of the change, and ironically we look to it also to help us cope with complexity and the acceleration of change.

Within the broad and relatively stable curricular framework, we will need frequent adjustments. At present, we need to upgrade our approach to problem solving as described in Chapters 2 through 4. The new library research techniques presented in Chapters 9 and 10 go far beyond the card catalog and *Readers' Guide to Periodicals Literature*. The case for instruction in social statistics and data processing is put forth in Chapters 6–8.

The geometrically expanding world reservoir of information is inevitably subject to varying interpretations. When feminists screen information, they arrive at their conceptions of knowledge. When minorities screen the same information, they arrive at different conclusions. So also do supply-side economists and Marxist socialists. Having many options is a kind of freedom, but it is not easy to achieve both tolerance and conviction.

Given the nature of issues in the world today, it is important to understand that they fit no single discipline. Indeed, issues are multidimensional and demand attention that is multidisciplinary. Contemporary problems cut across the natural sciences, mathematics, history, the social sciences, and humanities. Inductive and deductive reasoning are common to all disciplines as are the rules for definition and classification. More curricular collaboration would benefit everyone.

> *Throwing more information at students does not necessarily constitute improved instruction.*

Schools are faced with two major challenges. The first is to gain access to the accelerating flow of information. The second is to learn what is worth doing with information in schools. We have learned that throwing money at social problems does not necessarily solve them. Money may be necessary but not sufficient. In a similar way, throwing more information at students does not necessarily constitute improved instruction. In this volume, we have heavily stressed access to information and, to a lesser degree, application of information. There is less to be said about the latter because the profession has not yet explored it thoroughly. We need hundreds of innovative teachers to tap into the information flow and determine how it can best be used. Some ventures will succeed and others fall short. The profession will gradually generalize the results. Another bulletin of the NCSS in a few years could well be devoted to techniques of using information in various social studies subjects and levels.

Instructional Materials and Equipment

The primary flow of information and knowledge in the classroom is currently from the teacher and textbook to the students. Both of these sources respond slowly to changing information at a time when the flow of information in society is rapidly accelerating. Weekly student periodicals such as *Scholastic Update* offer one approach to timeliness. So also do on-line data bases. Business people have long used the "economic indicators" published frequently by the government. Now emerging are political, social, and environmental indicators. Few of these are suitable for students in their current form but special versions could readily be devised for social studies instruction. For example, each year the U.S. State Department publishes a record of how often each nation in the United Nations voted in agreement with the United States on ten key issues. This is an excellent indicator of the standing that our nation has with other nations. Mapping and comparing results from year to year make a good lesson that can be used as early as in the study of nations in the 6th and 7th grades. There are dozens of similar indicators that relate to every social studies subject. To make this kind of lesson practical requires some agency to assemble the data and put them into teachable form. Dissemination via an on-line data base would have many advantages. Perhaps this is a job for ERIC or the National Council for the Social Studies. In the local school, the library media specialist can be helpful in gaining access to data bases and other specialized information. Recent school library publications make the same point put forth by Callison in Chapter 9 that library media specialists want to play a more prominent role in curriculum planning and instruction in all subject areas. Many of them have the training necessary to make new kinds of information available in a practical way in the social studies classroom.

> *There should be at least one computer, a printer, and projection panel plus basic software in every social studies classroom.*

In Chapter 11 of this volume, Moseley makes a strong case that textbooks "still appear to be the most convenient and least expensive medium available" and are not likely to be supplanted by computer programs. We, the editors, agree that textbooks perform important instructional functions in an admirable way and are not likely to be replaced by any information technology described in this volume. Textbooks are excellent in presenting orderly exposition of subject matter in an understandable form. Most textbooks emphasize the concepts and generalizations designated by scholars as most important. Publishers may anguish over conflicting demands of factions, but on the whole, they are evenhanded. Teachers' manuals suggest several approaches to instruction and always recommend more than read, recite, and recall. If teachers fall into the bad habits, it is not the publishers' fault. Contrary to common opinion, we editors find most textbooks attractive in appearance and often interesting in content.

On the other side of the ledger, textbooks have two limitations that relate to an Information Age. First, the normal timetable of the life of a textbook in a local district results in the use of books that may be five to ten years old. With rapidly changing topics, this is far too long. Second, textbooks are not a good medium for raw data that students can use in inquiry. Data in the form of primary sources for student interpretation were popular in the 1960s but soon fell from favor for a variety of reasons. We believe that quality expository textbooks could be integrated with a data base to provide data processing experiences to students in ways that would reduce the major shortcomings responsible for inquiry's earlier shortcomings.

There should be at least one computer, a printer, and projection panel plus basic software in every social studies classroom. A modem in the library media center can serve the whole school but it will not be of much use unless there is a budget for on-line information services. The emergence of CD-ROM resources offers exciting new possibilities that merit investigation. All of these will cost money but are likely to prove important in preparing students for life in a rapidly changing society. With information technology appearing in business, manufacturing, government, sports—virtually everywhere we look—how can it remain so scarce in social studies classrooms?

The Teacher

The information explosion and the use of newer technologies call for a different mind-set on the part of the teacher. While teachers must continue to be well prepared and well informed, they cannot match the volume and variety of information and knowledge available from other sources. As defined in Chapter 9, the teacher's role becomes that of a mediator who creates the setting in which students reflect on the most significant issues in their lives as well as conditions in larger society. Wisdom is an elusive idea involving both intellectual and emotional dimensions. Wisdom is probably caught more than taught, and teachers seem to be a more likely source than any data base.

While teachers must continue to be well prepared and well informed, they cannot match the volume and variety of information and knowledge available from other sources.

Many, if not most, social studies teachers have been reluctant to use the new information technologies. Those who had an early exposure were often disappointed with the software and concluded that computers were only appropriate in mathematics and commercial subjects. In the last couple of years, social studies software has improved significantly in variety and quality, and this should continue as time passes. Our profession has its share of technophobes who may never be comfortable with a computer but most of the nonusers just need easy access and a little encouragement to get started. The great number of reluctant teachers who are nearing retirement should understand that a personal decision to avoid computers means that another decade of students will lack skills they need in life. Even more disturbing are the thousands of newly certified teachers who have not been introduced to educational technology nor to the application of mathematical knowledge to social issues.

Human Dimensions of the Information Age

"Maybe we can slip by without getting involved."

The great number of reluctant teachers who are nearing retirement should understand that a personal decision to avoid computers means that another decade of students will lack skills they need in life.

Finally, we offer some words of caution. Cameron Moseley recounts previous "trips down the garden path" with programmed instruction, inquiry, and a half dozen other curriculum breakthroughs. Moseley does not completely rule out the possibility that computers can help students work "smarter" but he adopts a show-me stance. In the light of the results of curriculum changes in the last couple of decades, his call for caution is well taken.

The Information Age with its attendant complexity offers great promise. But as we strike boldly out into complexity with our computers, CD-ROM, and modems close at hand, let us remember that the highest form of wisdom may be the Golden Rule. The most important lessons in school may be to practice courtesy and concern for others.